T0382154

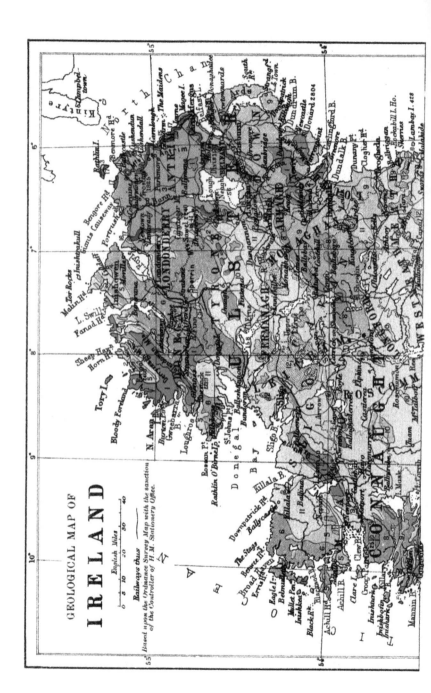

GEOLOGICAL MAP OF

IRELAND

English Miles

0 5 10 20 30 40

Railways thus

Based upon the Ordnance Survey Map with the sanction
of the Controller of H.M. Stationery Office.

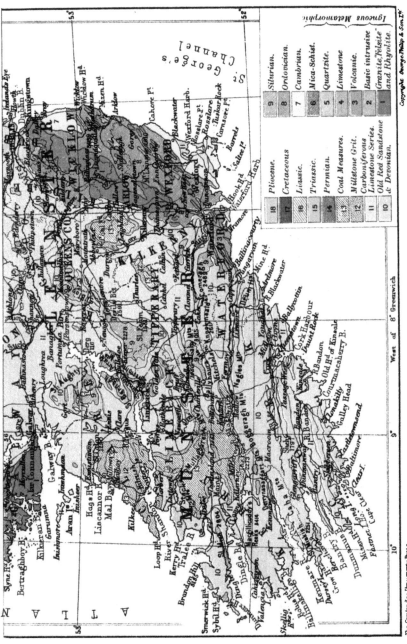

18	Pliocene.	9	Silurian.
17	Cretaceous.	8	Ordovician.
16	Liassic.	7	Cambrian.
15	Triassic.	6	Mica-Schist.
14	Permian.	5	Quartzite.
13	Coal Measures.	4	Limestone.
12	Millstone Grit.	3	Volcanic.
11	Carboniferous Limestone Series.	2	Basic intrusive.
10	Old Red Sandstone & Devonian.	1	Granite, Felsite and Rhyolite.

Igneous
Metamorphic

THE PROVINCES OF IRELAND

Edited by

GEORGE FLETCHER, F.G.S., M.R.I.A.

CONNAUGHT

CONNAUGHT

Edited by

GEORGE FLETCHER, F.G.S., M.R.I.A.

With Maps, Diagrams and Illustrations

CAMBRIDGE
AT THE UNIVERSITY PRESS
1922

CAMBRIDGE
UNIVERSITY PRESS

University Printing House, Cambridge CB2 8BS, United Kingdom

Cambridge University Press is part of the University of Cambridge.

It furthers the University's mission by disseminating knowledge in the pursuit of education, learning and research at the highest international levels of excellence.

www.cambridge.org
Information on this title: www.cambridge.org/9781107511361

© Cambridge University Press 1922

First published 1922
First paperback edition 2015

A catalogue record for this publication is available from the British Library

ISBN 978-1-107-51136-1 Paperback

EDITOR'S NOTE

THE aim of this series is to offer, in a readable form, an account of the physical features of Ireland, and of the economic and social activities of its people. It deals therefore with matters of fact rather than with matters of opinion; and, for this reason, it has happily been found possible to avoid political controversy. Ireland deserves to be known for her varied scenery, her wealth of archæological and antiquarian lore, her noble educational traditions, and her literary and artistic achievements. The progress and status of Ireland as an agricultural country are recognised and acknowledged, but her industrial potentialities have, until recently, been inadequately studied. The causes of the arrested development of her industries have been frequently dealt with. Her industrial resources, however, demand closer attention than they have hitherto received; their economic significance has been enhanced by modern applications of scientific discovery and by world-wide economic changes. It is hoped that these pages may contribute to the growing movement in the direction of industrial reconstruction.

It is unusual to enlist the services of many writers in a work of modest dimensions, but it was felt that the more condensed an account, the more necessary was it to secure authoritative treatment. It is hoped that the names of the contributors will afford a sufficient guarantee that the desired end has been achieved. The editorial task of co-ordinating the work of these contributors has been made light and agreeable by their friendly co-operation.

The scope of the volumes and the mode of treatment adopted in them suggest their suitability for use in the higher forms of secondary schools. A notable reform is in course of accomplishment in the teaching of geography. The list of place-names is making room for the more rational study of a country in relation to those who dwell in it, and of these dwellers in relation to their environment.

G. F.

Dublin, *January* 1922

POSTSCRIPT.

The traditional spelling *Connaught* has been retained in this volume for convenience, although it no longer expresses the true pronunciation of the name of the Province. As is explained on page 1, the *gh* should not be silent (as in the word *naught*): it represents a guttural like the *ch* in *loch*. The Irish spelling is *Connacht,* or preferably the plural form *Connachta,* that is *Conn-achta,* "the peoples descended from Conn." This division of the syllables should be noted in pronunciation.

CONTENTS

ILLUSTRATIONS

MAPS AND DIAGRAMS

The illustrations on pp. 11, 25, 32, 34, 35, 36, 37, 40, 93, 109, 126, 128, 133, 135, 145, 148, 149, 156 are from photographs by Valentine & Sons, Ltd.; those on pp. 39, 111, 113, 122, 123, 127 are reproduced by permission of the Galway Archæological and Historical Society; those on pp. 77, 85 are from photographs by Mr R. Welch; that on p. 144 from a photograph by Mr G. Fletcher; and that on p. 159 from a photograph by Mr T. F. Geoghegan.

Acknowledgments are due to the Department of Agriculture and Technical Instruction for Ireland, and to the Royal Irish Academy for permission to use illustrations which have appeared in their publications.

CONNAUGHT

ANCIENT GEOGRAPHY

THE oldest source of information that we possess regarding the ancient geography of Ireland is contained in the work of the second-century Alexandrian Ptolemy.

He gives fewer names for the region now called the province of Connaught [1] than for any of the other provinces of Ireland. He names three rivers, the *Libnios*, the *Ausoba*, and the *Senos*. The last should be the Shannon, by its name, though, if so, Ptolemy

[1] The spelling *Connaught* was good enough in its way when it was first invented, though it possesses no advantage over the proper native spelling *Connacht*. It is now, however, misleading, and might with advantage be abolished; for as English is now pronounced it tends to a slurring over of the guttural sound which is essential in the word (as in the English word *naught*; *i.e.* the name becomes *Con-nawt*, an ugly and meaningless corruption, instead of Conn-acht, its proper form). Similarly the spelling of *Lough* for *Loch* should be entirely abandoned, as well as the still worse *Knock* for *Cnoc* in the names of mountains. In the latter word the initial C should be sounded, but under the influence of the English word *knock* it has almost disappeared, thanks to the barbarous spelling now current. A further consummation devoutly to be wished for would be the wiping off from the map of the hideous prefix *Bally* (properly *Baile*); this, in a large proportion of the names in which it occurs, has no right to be there at all.

A

has erred in the position to which he has assigned it. The identification of the other rivers is not yet finally settled. He further names three tribes, the *Magnatai*, who seem to have occupied the north coasts of Mayo and Sligo, with a town *Magnata* (Moyne ? ?); the *Auteinoi*, with a town *Regia*; and the *Ganganoi* who appear to have inhabited Clare. All these names are very problematical. It is tempting to identify Magnata with the immense fort of Moghane in Clare, though such an identification would imply an unexampled blunder on Ptolemy's part; but it must be admitted that the omissions of Ptolemy are sometimes as inexplicable as the places he mentions.

The original territory of the *Connachta* was rather wider than the modern province of Connaught, in that it included the modern counties of Clare and Cavan, now reckoned to Munster and Ulster respectively. The chief tribal sub-divisions of the province were as follows : the *Ui Fiachrach*, reputed descendants of Fiachra, son of Eochu Muigmedon, king of Ireland A.D. 358–365 : in the north of Co. Mayo the *Conmaicne Mara*, one of several branches of the Conmaicne, or descendants of Conmac, son of Fergus and Medb, queen of Connaught : these inhabited the modern Connemara, which still preserves their name in a corrupt form : the regions called *Gno Mor* and *Gno Becc*, Great and Little Gno, west of Loch Oirbsen (now Loch Corrib). The tribe of the *Luigne* were situated in Co. Sligo ; the modern barony name of Leyney is a corruption of their name. The *Ciar-raige*, or descendants of Ciar, another son of Fergus and Medb, had territories in Mayo and Roscommon, as also in Munster, where they gave their name to the modern county of Kerry. The *Sil Muire-*

daig were an important sept in Roscommon; they were said to have been descended from Muiredach of Mag Ai, king of Connaught, who died A.D. 700; the O'Conors, Mac Dermots, and other local clans are derived from them. The *Ui Briuin*, descendants of Brian, king of Connaught, had various territories; the *Ui Briuin Breifni* or Ui Briuin of the territory called Breifne, occupied the modern counties of Leitrim and Cavan. The *Ui Maine Connacht*, so called to distinguish them from a similarly named tribe in what is now Westmeath, were a very important tribe occupying parts of Roscommon, Galway, Clare, and King's County. In the south of Galway, the modern barony of Kiltartan represents the ancient territory of Aidne, where a branch of the Ui Fiachrach were domiciled.

Connaught was granted to the De Burgos at the coming of the English; but like so many of the Anglo-Norman families, these developed sympathies with the Irish rather than with the English, and the province practically remained out of English jurisdiction altogether. Save that it seems to have been divided into two, called Connaught and Roscommon respectively, there was no attempt made to bring it under English forms of jurisdiction till the time of Elizabeth. Between 1566 and 1580 Sir Henry Sidney, the deputy, divided it for judicial purposes into shires, four in number; Leitrim, which was not subdued till 1583, was naturally not included in his scheme. Being anxious for administrative purposes to reduce the size of Munster, he annexed Thomond (*Tuad-Mumha*, North Munster) to this province, renaming it the County of Clare; it was however restored to Munster at the Restoration.

POPULATION

The people of the province of Connaught are the darkest in hair and eye of the inhabitants of Ireland. Even in Cong, Co. Galway, and its neighbourhood, where the fairest people in the province are to be found, the proportion of dark to fair is double that in Dublin. The darkest people recorded in Ireland are those of Clifden in Connemara. In stature the population of the south and west of Ireland are slightly taller on the average than those of the east and north. The *cephalic index* (see *Ireland* volume in this Series) ranges from 79.4 to 80.4. The heads of the Connaught people are distinctly broader than are those of the Munster men.

The Irish language as spoken in Connaught is characterised by a much more emphatic observance of the delicate distinctions between the pronunciation of the consonants with different vowel combinations than the Irish of the other provinces ; thus making the pronunciation of Irish more expressive and more musical in this province than elsewhere. The census returns show a decline in the language, due no doubt largely to the fact that it is Connaught and Munster which suffer most from the leakage of emigration. In 1891 there were 22,071 people in Connaught who could speak Irish only. This dropped in 1901 to 12,103, and in 1911 to 9367. The total number of speakers of Irish was 274,783, or 37.8 of the population, in 1891 ; in 1911 it was 217,087, or 35.5 of the population.

TOPOGRAPHY

The province of Connaught occupies the middle
portion of the western half of Ireland. Its northern
limit is marked by the line, founded on no conspicuous
natural features, which forms the northern and eastern
edge of Co. Leitrim, where it abuts on Ulster. The
southern limit is the sinuous southern boundary of
Co. Galway, where it marches with Munster. The eastern
end of both these lines rests on the Shannon, which
forms the eastern boundary.

Connaught as a whole is essentially a grazing country,
low limestone pasture prevailing in the inland parts
and mountain pasture and moor in the hilly marginal
areas.

Washed on three sides by the warm waters of the
Atlantic, over which sweep the prevailing winds, it has
a climate mild and insular in type—warm in winter,
cool in summer ; and condensation from the ocean
winds produces much cloud and rain. About half
the winds of the year are from the west (north-west to
south-west). As regards rainfall, the 40-inch line,
running north and south, corresponds roughly with
that of the Shannon—in other words with the eastern
edge of the province. Eastward the rainfall decreases,
westward it increases. The 50-inch line coincides
practically with the line of the Corrib-Mask-Conn chain
of lakes, which is also the eastern edge of the Galway-
Mayo highlands. A rainfall of 60 inches is reached
halfway across the mountain region, and in wet spots
among the hills west of this the precipitation reaches

70 or 80 inches, and probably more. On the most
westerly points of land—the islands lying off the coast
—the rainfall is not so great as on the adjoining hills
of the mainland. As regards temperature, the effect of
the ocean and the ocean winds is very marked. Frost,

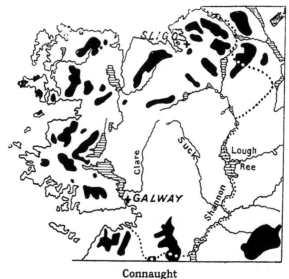

Connaught
(*Land over 500 feet elevation shown in black*)

almost unknown in the extreme west, is rare in the east.
In January, the isotherms of 40°, 41°, and 42° F. follow
one another in quick succession as one goes west from
the Shannon, the lines running nearly north and south.
In July, the warmest month, on the other hand, the
temperature falls as one goes west from the Shannon,
from 60° to 58° F. along the coast. The amount of
cloud is great, and the degree of humidity high. Along

the coast the rainfall is distributed over more than two-thirds of the days of the year. The vegetation bears witness in many ways to the permanence of moist conditions, and the constant bend of the trees towards the east, even in the Shannon valley, keeps one in mind

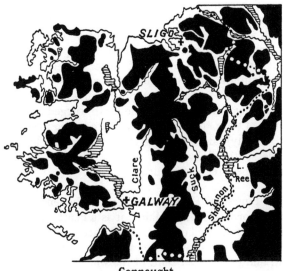

Connaught

(*Land over 250 feet elevation shown in black*)

of the prevalence and force of the westerly winds, which in the maritime districts renders the growth of trees impossible except where some local shelter prevails.

For topographical purposes Connaught may be divided into two regions. If from the Shannon we draw two lines due west, one to Galway Bay and one to Clew Bay, and draw a third line joining the heads of these two bays, we enclose a vast area of limestone plain, comprising the

County of Roscommon and the eastern parts of Galway and Mayo. Throughout this region, which comprises some 2500 square miles, only a couple of points rise above 500 feet, and most of the area lies below 250 feet. Grazing land predominates largely. Towards the west the soil becomes very thin, and the limestone comes to the surface with increasing frequency, till along the Corrib-Mask line of lakes the bare grey rock, fantastically carved by the dissolving rain, lies open to the sky over large areas. Sweeping in a semi-circle round this plain the rest of the province presents a great variety of hill-forms—flat-topped cliff-walled limestone hills in Sligo and Leitrim in the north, rugged mountain-groups of slate, quartzite, and granite in the west (Mayo and Galway), and strange grey ranges of bare limestone in the south (Galway and Clare). We shall now take each of these regions in turn.

The Limestone Plain is not a plain in the sense in which Holland or Norfolk is a plain ; it is a gently undulating tract, generally well drained, the surface occupied mainly by grassland and peat bog—grass occupying nearly 60 per cent. and peat 12 per cent. of the whole. The Shannon and its large tributary the Suck, flowing southward, drain the eastern half. A broad, low, barely perceptible watershed runs north and south down the middle of the area. The western half drains, mainly by the Rivers Clare and Robe, into the great chain of lakes—Carra, Mask, and Corrib—which lie along the western edge of the plain and find an outlet at Galway in the River Corrib. One of the most characteristic features of the area is the *turloughs*—depressions in the surface, often of considerable area, which are lakes in winter, and sweet green pasture in summer. These are filled by underground channels in the limestone when rains raise the general level of the subsoil waters, and are emptied by the same means when drier weather prevails.

Another characteristic feature is furnished by the *eskers*—those curious winding green gravel-ridges left on the surface by the retreating ice of the Glacial period. By contrast with the flat country on which they extend they often assume a definite importance in the landscape, and from their fragrant thyme-clad slopes singularly extensive views are often obtained.

Towns are few and far between, and factories of any kind almost unknown ; the people's wealth is in horses, cattle, and sheep, and the principal occupation in the towns lies in supplying the wide surrounding areas with the necessities and simple comforts of rural life. The Shannon supplies a waterway along the eastern fringe of the district, and Lough Corrib along the western ; steamers run on both routes, carrying passengers and goods ; but excepting a short branch from the Shannon to Ballinasloe, no canal enters the area. Towards the south, the main line of the Midland Great Western Railway crosses westward from the Shannon at Athlone to the sea at Galway ; and the Mayo branch, running north-west from Athlone to the sea at Clew Bay, traverses the plain diagonally, and furnishes the traveller with an excellent epitome of its characters. The roads, being repaired with limestone (the only available rock) are generally bad—dusty in summer, sticky in winter, and rutty all the time.

MOUNTAINS

Beginning in the north, we find the hilly coastal area of broken and diversified country extending from the sea at Sligo eastward to the Erne basin, in which several mountain groups of different type may be distinguished.

Fronting the Atlantic boldly between Sligo and Bundoran, Ben Bulben and its companions stand up conspicuously. These hills are formed of horizontal beds of limestone. Their surface, still retaining much of its ancient levelness, forms an undulating table-land 1000 to 2000 ft. above the surrounding country; their edges, where the onslaughts of weather have been aided by series of natural vertical cracks (" joints ") are boldly precipitous. Not only has the exposed western face been carved into imposing cliffs by rain and wind, but, aided by stream action, the forces of denudation have carved two deep gashes through the centre of the mass, forming the lovely cliff-walled valleys of Glencar and Glenade. This area is exceedingly picturesque, and has a special interest for the botanist, on account of the variety of alpine plants which cling to the cliff-walls. Southward, across the beautiful Lough Gill, dark knobby heathery hills contrast with the green grassy slopes of the limestone. The difference is due to change of rock: these hills are a continuation of the great Ox Mountains ridge, which will be mentioned presently. Eastward, the limestone hills continue, but are soon replaced by others of shale and sandstone, which reach their culmination in Slieveanieran (1922 ft.) overlooking Lough Allen. The name signifies the Mountain of Iron, from the occurrence there of iron ore, which was formerly mined extensively. These hills have none of

Near Ben Bulben, Sligo

the charm of Ben Bulben ; they are heathery and bare,
and the streams muddy and stained with iron.

The Ox Mountains form a high dark ridge running

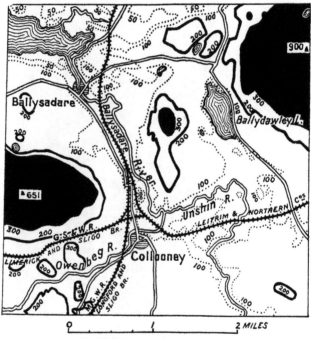

The Collooney Gap, Co. Sligo

south-west from Lough Gill in Sligo to Lough Cullin
in Mayo, the western end being known as Slieve Gamph ;
the highest point (Knockachree) is 1778 ft. They are
formed of very ancient rocks, are thickly clad with
bog, and possess few points of interest to the traveller.

In a length of 18 miles, the main ridge is crossed by only two roads, which rise to over 900 ft. and over 1000 ft. respectively.

The eastern continuation of these hills to Lough Gill, where they link up with those of the Ben Bulben group, would seriously bar the road to Sligo from Dublin and the south were it not for the presence of a narrow gap in the ridge at the little town of Collooney. Through this pass pours the Ballysadare River, which drains much of Co. Sligo ; many roads bound for Sligo also converge to this point ; and the three railways which connect with Sligo—from Limerick and the south, from Dublin and the centre, and from Enniskillen and the north, also all join at Collooney to use this natural gateway through the rocky hills. Its formation is no doubt due to the cutting action of the river, begun a very long time ago when the limestone plain stood higher than at present, and a notch in the hills here formed the natural line of drainage. As the level of the plain slowly sank owing to solution of the limestone, the cutting action of the stream on the hard rocks in the gap kept pace with it, and is still going on as the plain gradually becomes lowered by the agents of denudation.

A remarkable chain of lakes—Loughs Corrib, Mask, Carra, Cullin and Conn—running northward from Galway to Killala Bay, separates the limestone plain of Connaught from a very different district—a rough heathy area of moor and mountain—which forms West Mayo and West Galway. The change is due to a change of rock, the limestone giving place to ancient granites, quartzites, and slates. These rocks have resisted the ceaseless onslaught of the ocean, and still stand out boldly as a great buttress, though carved into innumerable headlands, bays, and islands. Many mountain groups rise within this region from among wide-extending lowland moors and bogs. North of Clew Bay, which, with the low limestone trough which continues eastward from it, divides the area into two parts, the Nephinbeg range rises to 2369 ft., and more to the eastward, Nephin, a huge dome of quartzite, reaches 2646 ft. On the southern shore of Clew Bay the beautiful cone of Croaghpatrick, crowned by a little chapel, towers to 2510 ft. South of this again there is a tangled mass of peaks grouped round the remarkable fiord of Killary Harbour—on the north side Mweelrea (2688 ft.), Sheffry (2504 ft.) and their neighbours, on the south the knobby ridge of Maam Turc (2307 ft.) and the beautiful cluster of quartzite peaks which forms the Twelve Bens (corrupted into *Pins*) of Connemara, the loftiest point of which (Benbawn) reaches 2395 ft.

Stretching southward from the Twelve Bens to the Atlantic a remarkable low moorland extends, thickly studded with rock-basins occupied by little lakes, forming a network in which land and water play about equal parts. A similar type of ground is met with in the Outer Hebrides.

Looking southward from the Connemara moorland across Galway Bay, a very different type of scenery meets the eye. There, in northern Clare and the adjoining part of Galway, the limestone again prevails, but is raised into hills with an undulating sky-line of a height of about 1000 ft. Even from a distance of many miles, their unusual grey tint catches the attention ; and a nearer view reveals that this is due to the fact that the rock has no covering of grass or peat, but lies bare and naked mile after mile, from the summits down in many parts to sea-level. The greater part of this area, lying as it does in Clare, belongs to Munster, and, strictly speaking, is outside the district dealt with in the present volume. But as the traveller to Galway, the capital of Connaught, cannot fail to have his attention caught by these strange hills, and as he will probably visit them, a brief notice of them is allowable here.

This is a weird expanse, like the country of a dream, and full of contradictions which no dream could excel. Though it is apparently a mere waste of bare rock, yet it forms much prized pasture land, on account of the sweet grass that fills every chink of the rock. Though it is watered by no streams—for the rain sinks at once down innumerable fissures in the rock—yet the vegetation is verdant, being nourished by the wet Atlantic winds. And here, where frost is almost unknown, we find plants which belong to the higher Alps and to the Arctic regions growing in sheets down to sea-level, mixed with others whose nearest station is on the sunny shores of the Mediterranean. The Burren, as this region is called, is one of the most interesting and curious areas in Ireland.

A lake-strewn plain of limestone separates the Burren hills from Slieve Aughty, a broad heathy mass of slates and sandstones which extends from South Galway into Clare. As one passes in the train from Ballinasloe to Galway, Slieve Aughty is conspicuous to the southward as a long featureless ridge. These hills are bare and desolate, and possess little of interest to the traveller. On the east they slope down to the Shannon, thus completing the semicircle of mountains which, commencing in Leitrim in the north, encloses the Connaught plain.

LAKES AND RIVERS

Connaught is abundantly supplied with lakes; these are mostly associated with the hills, or they occur on the edges of the plain. The great lakes of the Shannon, which bounds the province on the east, belong partly to Connaught—Loughs Derg, Ree and Allen and the groups of smaller sheets of water around Boyle and Dromod. Excepting Lough Allen, all of these lie in basins of limestone, and have been formed by the solvent action on that rock of water containing carbon dioxide. The solution of the limestone has proceeded very unevenly, and hence great irregularities as regards both conformation and depth are found. The lime-stone lakes are full of promontories, bays, and islands, and their bottoms of cliffs and pinnacles, as shown by the abrupt changes in soundings. These features apply still more to the great group of limestone lakes which fringe the plain on the west—Loughs Corrib, Mask, Carra, and Conn: on Lough Corrib especially boating is rendered dangerous by the number of reefs of rock which rise abruptly from deep water. Lough Corrib, the largest of the Connaught lakes, has a length of 26 miles, the breadth is most variable: the lake is deepest at its northern end, where soundings of 152 ft. have been obtained. At its north-western end a narrow arm penetrates far into the metamorphic hills of Connemara. The lake narrows half-way along its length, and here a ferry (Kilbeg Ferry) provides com-munication between the Headford district and that of Oughterard.

Lough Mask is more open than Lough Corrib, and rather deeper (191 ft.), it has the high dark ridge of

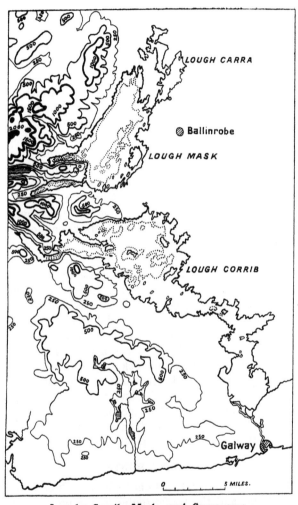

LOUGH CARRA

⊘ Ballinrobe

LOUGH MASK

LOUGH CORRIB

Galway

0   5 MILES.

Loughs Corrib, Mask, and Carra area

B

the Partry Mountains impending over it on the west. Lough Carra is a delightful mazy lake, with wonderfully clear water (due to springs) and a white bottom formed of a soapy calcareous deposit. Lough Conn has for its main feature the towering form of Nephin, which rises over the lake to a height of 2646 ft. Of the innumerable smaller lakes which diversify the province, a few must be specially commended for their beauty—Lough Inagh and its companions at the foot of the Twelve Bens, Lough Nafooey near Leenane, Lough Key and Lough Arrow near Boyle, and Lough Gill near Sligo.

The Shannon, which has already been referred to repeatedly, flowing along the edge of the province, drains its eastern third. The Corrib-Mask chain of lakes is an important drainage channel, receiving from the plain on the east several considerable streams, and from the west shorter and more rapid streams from the hills. From Lough Mask, which lies 36 ft. higher than Lough Corrib, the water passes by subterranean passages through the intervening barrier of limestone into the latter lake. At the lower end of Lough Corrib, the River Corrib has a broad, placid course of 5 miles, and then plunges suddenly over a low rock ledge through the city of Galway to the sea. In the north-west the Moy drains a considerable area of country, and, receiving the surplus waters of Lough Conn, flows northward to the sea at Ballina. The Sligo and Leitrim area is drained by a number of streams of less importance.

TRAFFIC ROUTES

Traffic into and out of Connaught has Dublin as its main focus, and the traffic routes of the province converge towards that point. Towards the east, in which direction Dublin lies, the Central Plain extends almost unbroken, far beyond the confines of the province, and the lines of thoroughfare are not diverted by natural barriers ; their course has been dictated by the positions of the towns, whose traffic requirements they are called upon to satisfy.

The province is served mainly by the Midland Great Western Railway. This line, running westward from Dublin, branches at Mullingar and again at Athlone, and sends across Connaught three diverging thoroughfares. The most southern of these is the main line to the port of Galway, which was extended some twenty years ago westward across Connemara for 49 miles to Clifden. North of this, the Mayo branch runs from Athlone W.N.W. to the port of Westport at the head of Clew Bay, and an extension continues to Achill Sound. More to the north the Sligo line, coming from Mullingar, crosses the Shannon and enters the Province at Drumsna, and runs N.N.W. to the port of Sligo through the interesting Collooney gap, which has been referred to already. A branch of the Mayo line runs north from Manulla to Killala, furnishing a fifth point at which this system penetrates to the Atlantic. Cutting across the lines of the M.G.W system, an important route, the extension of the old Waterford and Limerick Railway, runs south from Sligo across the province ; and Collooney, Claremorris, and Athenry, the points where it cuts the three M.G.W. routes, thus become important junctions. This line is now worked by the Great Southern and Western Railway. Finally, a line running through picturesque hills connects Sligo with Enniskillen on the east, and thence with the Ulster system.

The grasslands and moors of Connaught do not conduce to a large population or to heavy traffic. Trains are comparatively few and slow, and scenery tame until the western fringe of mountainous country is entered, as on the Connemara and Achill extensions, where glorious views unfold themselves to the traveller.

Canals are nearly as rare in Connaught as snakes in Iceland. Save for a line of 15 miles continuing the Grand Canal from the Shannon to Ballinasloe, and another a mile long connecting Lough Corrib with the sea at Galway, the only artificial waterways inside the province are found in Leitrim, where the canal which joins the rivers Erne and Shannon runs across the county from near Carrick-on-Shannon. As already mentioned, the Shannon itself, running along the eastern edge of the province, is an important waterway, and occasional artificial diversions occur where obstacles in the river interfere with navigation. Near Cong, on the barrier of limestone which separates Lough Mask from Lough Corrib, an instructive example of futile engineering may be seen. The stream which flows between the two lakes runs underground through passages which it has dissolved out of the soluble rock. It was proposed to make a canal between the two lakes, and the canal was constructed and is there still—but it is empty. The water when admitted disappeared immediately through innumerable fissures in the rocky floor, and the work had to be abandoned.

ROUND THE COAST

The coast of Connaught as a whole forms a great projecting buttress, standing boldly out from the general line of the western shore of Ireland. The deeper indentations of the coast line—Sligo Bay, Killala Bay, Clew Bay, and Galway Bay—all coincide with areas of limestone, and are no doubt largely due to solution of the rock. The straight east-and-west lines which form the northern and southern edges of the buttress— running respectively from Sligo to Broad Haven and from Galway to Kilkieran Bay—are believed to be due to old fractures of the earth's crust. Stretching between the two east-and-west lines aforesaid, the west coast of the province is carved into a thousand bays, promontories, and islands.

Beginning in the north, the County of Leitrim fronts Donegal Bay for a distance of only 3 miles. South of this, the coast of Sligo, trending generally southwest, has for its main feature the wide bay of Sligo, which divides into three shallow, land-locked inlets, the bays of Drumcliff, Sligo, and Ballysadare. The central branch, at the head of which lies Sligo town, alone is used as a waterway. A channel, which hugs the northern shore of the inlet, allows steamers of considerable tonnage to reach the quays at Sligo, which are connected with the railway system.

Sligo, now a bustling town, occupies the site of an important ford of earlier days. The coastwise road must at all times have been a notable thoroughfare here, for high hill masses bar the route from north to south save close to the ocean. At Sligo the River Garvogue falls over edges of rock into the sea. Eastward, its course is deep and broad to where it flows from Lough Gill, which continues the water-barrier for six more miles to the eastward, deep among the hills. All north-and-south traffic therefore had to cross the ford at Sligo, and at this important point a town sprang up. The position of the ancient ford is still clearly indicated by the old bridge which spans the shallowest part of the stream, carrying the main road from Dublin and the south across the river beside the Imperial Hotel.

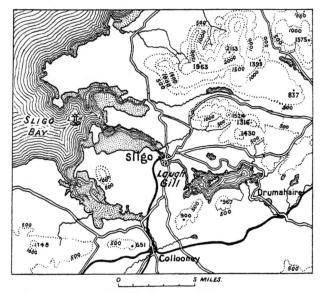

The Environs of Sligo

From Sligo a rather uninteresting coast-line, backed by the gloomy Ox Mountains, trends westward to Killala Bay, which is wide and sandy, with the villages of Inishcrone and Killala on its eastern and western sides, and the sandbank of Bartragh Island almost blocking the bay between. Here is the mouth of the River Moy, up which the tide flows for seven miles to where stands the little town of Ballina, the marketing centre for a vast and sparsely inhabited district lying to the westward. Here we are again on a line of railway, a branch of the Midland Great Western system. A few miles to the south-west is Lough Conn, with the great mass of Nephin towering over it. At Ballina we pass from Co. Sligo into Co. Mayo.

From Killala Bay the coast continues westward for 25 miles to Broad Haven. Cliffs begin almost at once, at Downpatrick Head, where horizontal ledges of rock provide a home for breeding sea-birds. Beyond the little inlet of Belderg the cliffs become lofty and thence westward the coast scenery is magnificent, with stupendous precipices and bold outlying stacks, tenanted in summer by myriads of birds. A couple of miles out to sea, the Stags (*i.e.* Stacks) of Broad Haven, a series of splintered pinnacles, rise out of the ocean. In Broad Haven the scenery becomes less imposing, and a shallow inner bay leads up to Belmullet.

The Mullet is a peninsula shaped like the head of a hammer, 15 miles in length. It is a wind-swept, wild, flattish area covered with peat and sand, and is joined to the mainland by an isthmus only three hundred yards wide, through which a canal has been cut, permitting of the passage of boats from Broad Haven on the northern side to Blacksod Bay on the southern. Standing on the isthmus is the little town of Belmullet, the name signifying the mouth or entrance of the Mullet. A mile below the town a pier allows of the berthing of a small steamer which runs every second day along the coast to Sligo. Otherwise communication with the outer world is maintained by the mail car, which runs daily to Ballina—42 miles by road.

South of Belmullet, a wild, low bogland intersected with shallow arms of the sea extends for some 20 miles to Achill Island and the Curraun peninsula.

Achill Island is the largest island on the Irish coast, having an area of 57 square miles. Here again peat bog and mountain prevail, with only occasional patches of

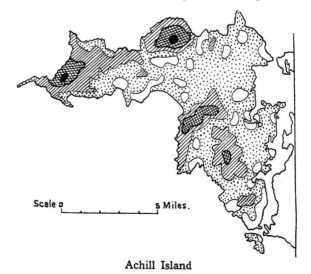

Achill Island

Cultivated areas, white; Bogland up to 500 ft., dotted; to 1000 ft., hatched; 2000 ft., cross-hatched; over 2000 ft., black

poor cultivation. Two high hills (Slievemore 2204 ft., and Croaghaun 2192 ft.) dominate the island; there is imposing cliff scenery, Croaghaun descending into the ocean in one huge precipice; and the island is, as it deserves to be, a favourite resort of visitors.

A shallow, narrow, winding channel, now crossed

Slievemore, Achill Island

by a swing-bridge, separates Achill from the Curraun peninsula, or Curraun Achill, a lofty moorland which connects with the mainland by a narrow neck at Mallaranny, another tourist resort, through which the railway from Achill passes on its way to Westport.

Clew Bay, which now intervenes, is a deep, somewhat rectangular indentation in the coast, some 20 miles long by 8 or 10 miles broad. The depression which forms it is continued on land eastward till it merges with the Central Plain. The basin is, in fact, due to the carving out by solution of a tongue of limestone, which runs westward from the plain with hill-masses of older rocks flanking it on north and south. The valley is choked with " drumlins," or whale-backed ridges of glacial drift, which are seen well as one goes from Westport to Newport ; and as its floor drops below sea level, these stand up first as promontories and peninsulas, then as an archipelago, and finally, where the waves have completed their destruction, as reefs of boulders. The destruction of the islands by storms from the west may be studied to advantage on the outer fringe of the archipelago, where half of many of the islets has been removed, the stones from the vanished portion forming a great boulder-beach below a tall cliff of drift into which the sea is still cutting. The little towns of Westport and Newport lie among the drumlins at the head of the bay. Westport was, before the advent of railways, an important port. The valley which lies behind it is the only convenient entrance from the Atlantic into the Central Plain along a hundred miles of coast, for from Killala Bay to Galway Bay the barrier of mountain and bog is otherwise almost unbroken. But the advent of railways has shifted the distributing centres to Galway and Sligo, or more still to Dublin; and tall, empty warehouses remain to attest the former importance of Westport.

Half blocking the entrance of Clew Bay, Clare Island rises conspicuously. The island is noticeable from the lofty hill, 1520 ft. in height, which rises on its

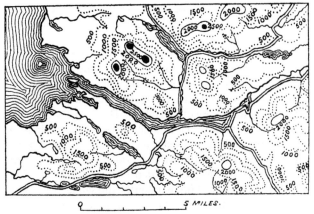

Killary Harbour and Mweelrea

north-western edge, and drops, like Croaghaun in Achill, into the Atlantic in a single grand precipice. South of Clare Island, many other islands fringe the coast right round to Galway Bay, the largest being Inishturk and Inishbofin. The last is the only one possessing a safe harbour, and is a fishing centre of some importance.

Resuming our coastal survey at Westport mention must be made of Croaghpatrick (2510 ft.) which rises in a beautiful cone over the southern shore of Clew Bay, and dominates the whole inlet. From the southern entrance of the bay, the land runs southward to the interesting fiord known as Killary Harbour—an inlet of extremely deep water, some 10 miles long and only half a mile wide, running far in among the mountains. It represents an ancient river-valley, now sunk beneath the waves, and deepened by glacial action. At its head, Leenane, well supplied with hotels, forms a delightful tourist centre.

Crossing Killary, we enter the western portion of Co. Galway, known as Connemara. The coast sweeps in a wide curve south-west and then south-east, and thence in a straight line far to the eastward to Galway City, lying at the head of Galway Bay. This coast-line is of a most intricate character, with innumerable headlands, bays and islands, bare and windswept, and beaten upon incessantly by the Atlantic rollers. In the extreme west, the little town of Clifden lies snugly at the head of a narrow bay, and further south, the village of Round-stone has a more commodious and safer harbour, and a considerable fishing industry.

Lying off the entrance of Galway Bay, long, low, and grey, are the three islands of Aran—Inishmore, Inish-maan, and Inisheer. They belong politically to Galway, but naturally to Clare, being outlying reefs of the gaunt limestone hills that form the Burren district. They are mere bare ribs of rock, on which arable land has been produced by the industry of the islanders, who for generations have carried up sand and seaweed on their backs to lay on the " fields." Fuel is entirely absent from the islands, and for their firing the people rely on the bogs of Connemara, from which district an abundant supply of peat is obtained. On Inishmore, which is by far the largest island of the group (length 8½ miles) an excellent harbour (Killeany Bay) is available, and here is situated the principal village of the islands (Kilronan).

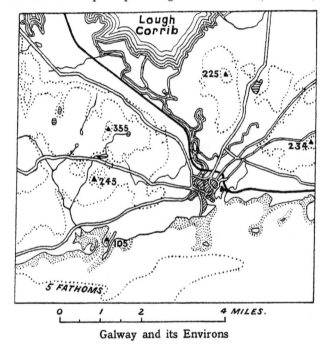

Galway and its Environs

Much fishing is done from all the islands, chiefly in the light canvas-covered curraghs which are so much in use along the whole west coast of Ireland, and which are marvellously good sea-boats. In old days the Aran Islands harboured important ecclesiastical settlements, and the early Christian remains which still abound attract many students of archæology. Imposing remains of earlier races exist in the form of massive forts of dry masonry, of great size and complicated design.

The city of Galway, the capital of Connaught, stands on the northern shore of the deep indentation of Galway Bay, close to its head. Its position resembles strikingly that of Sligo (see p. 22). In each case a lake-barrier, running far inland (in this case Lough Corrib, 26 miles in length), continued seaward as a deep unfordable stream, confines all coastwise traffic to a space a few hundred yards wide, where the river foams over limestone ledges into the sea, and is fordable. In addition boats can lie in shelter at the river-mouth. During the long period of raids and counter-raids, the ford of Galway, forming the gate to the whole of Connemara, was a post of first importance, and through it all westbound traffic must still pass, whether by road or rail. The next road westward lies over twenty miles to the north, across the tongue of land which divides Lough Corrib from Lough Mask, and thence through wild mountain valleys to Leenane, at the head of the Killary fiord.

South from Galway a low deeply-indented coast forms the head of Galway Bay to the borders of Clare, where the province of Munster begins.

COUNTIES AND TOWNS

Although the area of Connaught is as large as the average of the other three provinces, only five counties are included within it (as against an average of nine counties in each of the others). This arises from the exceptional size of Mayo and Galway. The counties are as follows :—

				Area in Square Miles.	Population (1911).
Leitrim .	.	.	.	613	63,582
Sligo	.	.	.	721	79,045
Roscommon	.	.	.	950	93,956
Mayo	.	.	.	2114	192,177
Galway .	.	.	.	2404	182,224
Total .	.	.	.	6802	610,984

Of these Roscommon is the only one which does not border on the Atlantic. Leitrim has a shore-line of only 3 miles ; Sligo, Mayo, and Galway have long and indented coasts.

Co. Leitrim

A long, narrow county, running from the sea at Donegal Bay far to the south-east. In the middle it is almost cut in two by Lough Allen, through which flows the infant Shannon. Around Lough Allen are high, dark hills (Slieveanieran, 1922 ft., and others), which yield coal and iron. South of these the county is low and undulating, with many small lakes. North of it hilly ground prevails—first dark heathery hills resembling Slieveanieran, but between Manorhamilton and the Atlantic table-topped limestone mountains (to 2113 ft.) bounded by lofty cliff-walls (see p. 10).

Carrick-on-Shannon, the assize town (1013), is on the south-western border, on the edge of the river, which is already of imposing size ; Mohill (755) is in the lake-strewn country to the south ; Manorhamilton (1013) is beautifully situated among the northern hills.

Co. Sligo

Three types of scenery are observed by the traveller through Co. Sligo. In the north, extending into Leitrim,

Markree Castle, Co. Sligo

a group of bold limestone hills, their tops forming a
plateau of an average of 1500 ft. in height (reaching
2113 ft. at its highest point), their edges forming lofty
grey cliffs, are a very striking feature. Across the
middle of the county, the high, dark ridge of the Ox
Mountains (1778 ft.), bare, and bog-covered, runs in a
south-westerly direction. Most of the rest of the
county is low limestone plain. The coast is indented
by several long, sandy inlets. Several very beautiful
lakes lie among hills in the north and east. Drainage
northward toward the sea is blocked by the long range
of the Ox Mountains. The Moy, which drains most
of the west of the county, reaches the sea by outflanking
this barrier on the west. The Collooney River escapes
through a remarkable gap in the ridge, referred to
on pp. 12-13.

Sligo, the county town (11,163), is a bright and busy
place, situated on an important old ford (see p. 21).
It has very beautiful surroundings as regards sea, lake,
and mountain, and is a port with considerable traffic.
Ballymote (930) and Tobercurry (829), lying inland,
are market-towns, serving large districts. Collooney,
near Sligo, has the advantage of plenty of water-power,
in the falls of the Ballysadare River.

Co. Roscommon

An inland, low-lying area (98 per cent. of the surface
being under 500 ft. elevation), formed almost entirely
of drift-covered limestone. The few hills which occur
lie on the edges of the northern part of the county—
Slieve Bane (857 ft.) on the east, and the Curlew Hills
(863 ft.) and the Bralieve group (1377 ft.) in the north.
The county is drained by the Shannon and the Suck,

c

The River Garvogue at Sligo

the first forming the whole eastern boundary, and the second much of the western. The west side of Lough Ree belongs wholly to Roscommon, further north are various smaller expansions of the Shannon ; and on the north and north-west edges many other lakes, including the beautiful Lough Key, belonging wholly

Main Street, Roscommon

to the county. Grazing land occupies nearly 60 per cent. of the surface. Towns are few.

Roscommon, the county town (1858), is chiefly interesting to the antiquary. Boyle (2691) is prettily situated on a swift stream at the foot of the Curlew Hills. Castlerea (1224) stands on the Suck. Ballaghaderreen (1317) far to the west. Part of Athlone belongs to this county.

Co. Mayo

Mayo is a very large county with a great variety of scenery—wide plains and wild mountains, large lakes, rushing rivers, huge sea cliffs, and rocky, storm-swept islands. The north-and-south line formed by the

Market Place, Ballina

chain of large lakes—Mask, Carra, Cullin, and Conn—roughly divides the county into a lowland and an upland area—nearly all the land to the eastward being low, grassy limestone country, and nearly all west of the line being mountainous and heathery, and formed of old metamorphic rocks, with slates in the south. The higher hills, usually from 2000 to 2500 ft. in elevation, rise either singly, like Nephin, Croaghpatrick, and the two high peaks of Achill ; or in groups, like the Nephinbeg range, the Partry Mountains, and the Mweelrea group.   The coast is exceedingly broken and wild, with large inlets, promontories, peninsulas, and many islands, of which Achill (the largest Irish island), Clare Island, and Inishturk are the chief.   The cliff-scenery

Turlough Village, Mayo

of the north coast is magnificent.   The north-western part of the county forms a vast, almost unbroken bog-land.   Clew Bay is remarkable on account of the way in which the hummocky limestone ground at its head dips slowly down below the sea, producing an archipelago of grassy islands.   The rivers are short, the Moy, flowing into Killala Bay, being the only considerable stream within the county.

The coast is almost devoid of towns, Westport (3674), at the head of Clew Bay, being the only one of any importance ; it has good harbour accommodation, but the spread of railways has tended to curtail its sea-borne trade. Ballina (4662) is on the Moy, a few miles above its mouth. Belmullet (681), on a narrow peninsula far to the north-west, is one of the most remote spots in Ireland. Castlebar (3698), the assize town, stands near the centre of the county. Eastward in the plain are Swineford (1302), Claremorris (1069) (an important railway junction), and Ballinrobe (1585), near Lough Mask.

Co. Galway

Next to Cork, Galway is the largest county in Ireland, having the size of three average counties. Even more than in Mayo, we find in Galway a striking contrast between the eastern and western parts of the area, and for the same reason—in the east limestone prevails, now worn down to a low-lying, grassy plain ; while in the west—that is, west of Lough Corrib, which divides the county into two parts—are ancient hard metamorphic rocks, which have resisted the weather, and form hummocky lowlands, covered with bog and starred with lakes, or rise in tall, bare hills to a height of over 2000 ft. (see p. 13). A lower range, Slieve Aughty (1207 ft.), rises on the southern border of the county. The eastern boundary is formed by the Suck and the Shannon, including the greater part of Lough Derg. The north-eastern plain is drained by the Clare-Galway River, which flows into Lough Corrib. That great lake, 26 miles in length, with sinuous shores and innumerable islets and reefs, lies on the western edge of the plain, and the brown hills of Connemara rise on its western side. Connemara (or Galway west of Lough Corrib) is filled with lakes, and ramifying sea-inlets and innumerable small islands accentuate the tangle of land and water. The Aran Islands, an outlying portion of the limestone hills of North Clare, belong politically to Galway : they are referred to on p. 28.

Galway (13,255), the capital of the province, stands near the head of Galway Bay on the narrow neck of land, crossed by the River Corrib, which intervenes between Lough Corrib and the sea. The River Corrib, draining not only the lake of that name but also Lough Mask, Lough Carra, and a large surrounding area, has a length of only 5 miles, and at Galway city foams down in rapids to meet the sea. There is a good

Inscribed Stone on Inchagoil, Lough Corrib

tidal dock, with accommodation for large vessels, but, like

most of the western towns, Galway has lost its importance as a distributing centre owing to the advent of railways. To the east, the main line of the Midland Great Western Railway runs across the Central Plain to Dublin, 126 miles. To the W.N.W. a recent extension leads through the heart of Connemara 49 miles to

" Spanish Arch," Galway

Clifden. Through the middle of the town the River Corrib, famous for its salmon fishing, rushes in its steep short descent from Lough Corrib to the sea. Ballinasloe (5169), on the River Suck, is famous for its great horse-fair. Athenry (791) was formerly a place of much importance. Loughrea (2388) is a market-town with a large trade. Portumna (873) lies on the Shannon, where that river enters Lough Derg. Gort (1166) is in the south-east, and Tuam (2980), an ancient and important ecclesiastical centre, in the north-east. Clifden (809), far away on the western coast, is the chief town of Connemara.

GEOLOGY

THE succession of strata in geological time, and their representation in Connaught, are shown in the following table :—

QUATERNARY		Bogs. Raised beaches. Glacial deposits.
CAINOZOIC.	Pliocene . Miocene. Oligocene . Eocene . .	Terrestrial conditions. Era of considerable denudation. Some volcanic action in the Eocene or Oligocene Period.
MESOZOIC.	Cretaceous . Jurassic . Triassic .	No traces ; but Cretaceous rocks occur beneath the Atlantic off the Mayo coast.
PALÆOZOIC.	Permian .	No traces.
	Carboniferous .	Coal Measures of Leitrim and Roscommon. Sandstone and Shale Series. Carboniferous Limestone Series, with sandstone and shale towards the base.
	Devonian .	Old Red Sandstone of Armorican upfolds.
	Silurian .	Cores of the Armorican upfolds. Llandovery to Ludlow beds of Killary Harbour.
	Ordovician .	Arenig to Bala ·beds of Killary Harbour.
	Cambrian .	Not recognised.
PRE-CAMBRIAN		Metamorphosed sediments and intrusive dolerites and granites of the Ox Mountains and Western Mayo and Galway.

Connaught, from the great plainland of Roscommon to the desolate mountain-bogs of Mayo and the grey rock-domes of Connemara, presents greater geological variety than either Leinster or Munster, and almost rivals Ulster in its scenic contrasts. The old Pre-Cambrian continent, remoulded on its margin by the Caledonian earth-movements at the close of Silurian times, is still revealed in the west of Galway and of Mayo, where it forms the mountain-land. Its crumpled rocks reappear along the Ox Mountains, and are never far from the surface under the limestone scarps of Sligo. The oldest rocks of the *Pre-Cambrian* region are, as is usually the case throughout the world, of sedimentary origin. We seem nowhere to reach down to the prim-ordial earth on which rain and rivers had not as yet begun to act. In Mayo and Connemara we find up-tilted quartzites, mica-schists, and occasional crystalline marbles, representing sandstones, clays, and limestones which were probably deposited in a sea. Dark masses of dolerite, now converted into hornblende-schist, penetrated them freely from below, and they became highly altered by pressure and by heating during the earliest folding movements. Granite welled up in the region, partly in Pre-Cambrian times and partly along the axes of Caledonian folding, and each molten mass absorbed part of the rocks above it in its advance. Some of the most important observations on the forma-tion of the crystalline rock known as banded gneiss were made in Connemara by Charles Callaway, who showed how dark pre-existing rocks may become streaked out in a viscid mass of invading granite.

The prevalence of sands among the old deposits of the west has greatly influenced the scenery of Galway

and Mayo. The resulting quartzites, though they have
not lost their stratification, are so firmly cemented by
silica that they break even through the original sand-

**Pre-Cambrian Quartzite. The Maam Turc Range,
Connemara**

grains. Abundant small joints, due to the cracking of
the rock when folded, allow the débris to stream down
in almost any direction from an upraised mass. The
quartzite crests thus become conical, and the Twelve

Bens of Connemara rise as great bare domes above milder lands of mica-schist (see p. 54). The Maam Turc Mountains to the east display a more regular scarp ; but the conical form is again excellently seen in Nephin above the waters of Lough Conn. Slievemore in Achill retains a crest of quartzite, and a similar capping, only recently worn away, probably determined the form of other mountains in the island. The cliffs of Minaun, south of Slievemore, are cut by the Atlantic in almost horizontal beds of quartzite. In their lower part they have become overfolded and contorted in a marked degree, where veins of very coarse granite, consisting mainly of red felspar and quartz, penetrate them from below. The igneous attack seems here responsible for a general weakening of the beds, and the consequent yielding and appearance of flow may be ascribed to heat rather than to earth-pressures. At the west end of Achill, the great cliff, descending 2000 ft. from the summit of Croaghaun, records, like Slieve League in Donegal, the stability of the ancient quartzites.

The occasional bands of limestone, which may represent marine precipitates rather than primordial shell-banks, are too full of crystalline silicates to be of use for lime-burning. At Streamstown, Ballynahinch, and Recess in Connemara, along an east-and-west line of strike, alteration by igneous rocks has converted the limestone and dolomite into a handsome serpentinous marble.

The altered Pre-Cambrian Irish series is classed with the *Dalradian* of A. Geikie, who placed under this convenient heading the crystalline rocks of Pre-Devonian but uncertain age that form so much of northern Ireland and of the Scottish highlands. Dalradian rocks extend

across Mayo, and the Ox Mountains represent a granitic
core, which has partly absorbed and partly intermingled
with the complex series of sediments in the earth-fold

Glaciated Slope of the Ox Mountain Range above a
Lowland of Carboniferous Limestone near Sligo

into which it rose. This long ridge stretches as a moorland above Castlebar and Sligo, and at its north end
often presents a glaciated surface of bare rock. An
important mass of coarse red granite, mingled with the

pre-existing schists, runs from Erris Head to Blacksod Point in Mayo, and forms a protective barrier between Blacksod Bay and the Atlantic waves.

Cambrian rocks are unknown in Connaught; but Arenig fossils have been found by J. R. Kilroe, R. G. Carruthers, and H. B. Maufe, near the head of Killary Harbour. The coarse conglomerates of Leenane, and the overlying slates in the south of Mayo, are in consequence now included in the lower part of the *Ordovician*; the barren grits, resting on Llandilo slates, that form the terraced masses of Mweelrea are of Llandilo or Bala age. These grits may have accumulated on a land-surface under dry conditions, while the sea occupied much of Ireland to the east. Erosion then set in; but the succeeding Llandovery, Wenlock, and Ludlow strata, recognisable in the country between Croaghpatrick and central Connemara, give a fairly complete *Silurian* system. The Silurian beds contain fragments of the metamorphosed rocks on which they lie, and the occurrence of granites and quartz-schists among the pebbles of the Arenig conglomerates still further emphasises the antiquity of the igneous and metamorphic rocks of Connemara.

The grand quartzite cone of Croaghpatrick, which dominates the scenery of Clew Bay, has been shown by J. R. Kilroe to be Silurian. There is thus a possibility of the discovery of other Silurian rocks among the quartzites of the heart of Mayo. Granite of Caledonian age penetrates the Llandovery strata south of Croaghpatrick, forming a marked ridge in a low moorland; and a long sheet of dark green serpentine has been intruded at the base of the Croaghpatrick series. This serpentine crops out also in the Ordovician and

Silurian block of Clare Island, which adds so picturesque
a feature to the wide entry of Clew Bay.

Old Red Sandstone occurs as a border to the Carboniferous exposures, making barren ground along the north

Cone of Croaghpatrick, Co. Mayo
Silurian Quartzite

shore of Clew Bay; as the long ridge of the Curlew Hills
above Boyle (see p. 52), where young Hugh O'Donnell's
army held the barrier against the English; and as the
dissected dome of Slieve Aughty in the south of Galway,
where moorland crests more than 1000 ft. in height look
down on the expanded River Shannon at Lough Derg.

Three inlying domes of Old Red Sandstonè rise through the plain between the Curlew Hills and central Galway, and are clearly due to the gentle swelling of the strata

Plateau of Ben Bulben, Co. Sligo
*Upper Carboniferous Limestone above shaly limestone.
Bogland of Grange in foreground*

under the Armorican folding at the close of Carboniferous times.

Sligo and Leitrim present a finer picture of the succession of Carboniferous strata than any other part of Ireland, though the basal shales and shaly limestones correspond to a horizon about the middle of the Lower

Carboniferous series. The upper limestone beds are far more pure, and weather out along their vertical joints in bold scarps and pinnacled walls. The softer strata below form steep slopes stretching to the valley-floors, and landslips from the upper terraces carry picturesque details into the lower ground. Glencar, opening north of Sligo town, possesses the attraction of the Derbyshire dales combined with that of nearness to the sea. The level crest of the great limestone plateau bears here and there relics of higher sandstones, such as the outlier on Truskmore, 2000 ft. above the sea. Sandstones also occur in the base of the series, indicating that we are near the shore of the sea that covered so much of Europe in Carboniferous times. They prevail again characteristically on the Millstone Grit horizons, and are succeeded by Lower Coal Measure shales and sandstones. This series remains on the hill-crests round Lough Allen, where coal is systematically mined in almost level strata. The fine limestone heights, rising 1000 ft. above Lough Arrow, are backed on the east by sombre hills of Upper Carboniferous strata, culminating in Slieveanieran and Bencroy, and contributing from their wet moorlands to the head-waters of the Shannon.

The site of Sligo town is of singular beauty. The bold scarp of the upper limestone dominates it on the north, and rises as an almost continuous wall above the coast-road to Bundoran. Lough Gill, close to the town, is bounded on the north by terraced Carboniferous limestone hills, and on the south by the bare grey termination of the Ox Mountains. From the crest of the gneissic ridge we may look east to the high Lough Allen coalfield, and south over the limestone

D

plain to the base of the Carboniferous system in Roscommon.

The county of Roscommon is typically plainland, rising to the historic plateau of Rathcroghan. One may travel 50 miles from the mouth of the River Suck to Boyle without encountering any hills except drumlins and glacial eskers. Grey limestone, almost a white " fossil marble," crops out here and there in level sheets amid thin grass. Bogs and boulder-clay are absent from a large part of the country, which is, no doubt, well drained beneath the surface, and the limestone forms a plateau 8 miles wide on the west bank of the broad valley of the Shannon. The plain continues across the great limestone surface westward, bearing drift and numerous isolated bogs, and is cut down somewhat by various streams flowing to the Atlantic at Galway Bay. The east sides of Lough Mask and Lough Corrib are low, and the water is still extending their borders by solution of the limestone. Their west sides, however, belong to the Pre-Cambrian and Silurian land, and the dark mountains of Maamtrasna rise steeply and strangely from a peneplain that stretches to the Irish Sea at Dublin. This vast surface represents the base-level to which the limestone land was worn down during Cainozoic times. Since then, it has been elevated through some 300 ft., and is again in course of denudation. The limestone reaches the Atlantic in Killala, Clew, and Galway Bays, and dredgings show that it once extended farther west. The Aran Islands of Co. Galway are almost soilless shelves, relics of the submerged plainland and threatened by the Atlantic waves. Clew Bay is a worn synclinal of Carboniferous strata into which the sea has been admitted. The whole coast, from Benwee Head in Mayo to St John's Point in Donegal, is merely a casual junction of sea and plain, beyond which the ridge of the Ox Mountains rises as a survival from the Caledonian land.

As is the case in a large part of Ireland, nothing is known of the *Permian* and *Mesozoic* history of Connaught. The frequent occurrence of Cretaceous flint, on the shores of Atlantic islets, or in dredgings off the western coast, suggests that chalk may have been laid down, not only in the Atlantic region, but also across part of the land to eastward. The next recorded event, however, after the late Carboniferous Armorican folding, and the formation of the peneplain on the continent of Cainozoic times, is the oncoming of the *Glacial* epoch.

The cold at first induced local glaciers on highlands such as those of Leitrim and Connemara ; but soon the main precipitation was concentrated in central Leitrim and Fermanagh. A great elongated snow-dome, spreading from the Lough Allen hills and Slieve Bawn as from a nucleus, generated ice that flowed north-westward into Donegal and Sligo Bays, crossing the Ox Mountains in the latter district (see p. 45), and south-westward and south-eastward over the limestone plain of Roscommon, Mayo, and Galway. The westerly extension of the southern glaciers reached Clew Bay, and left its deposits on Clare Island. From this or from a later ice-extension, numerous drumlins, elongated mounds of boulder-clay, were deposited in what is now a marine area. They resemble in Clew Bay the drumlins of Boston Harbour, Massachusetts, and the sea has carved out cliffs in them, which face outwards to the Atlantic. At the base of the "hundred islands" thus added to

Clew Bay, the floor of Carboniferous limestone may be sometimes seen, and the hummocky drift-covered land

The Curlew Hills, from Keshcorran, Co. Sligo
Drumlins in the intervening lowland

between Westport and Newport is merely an unsubmerged repetition of the bay.

Maxwell H. Close, who first traced out in 1866 the general directions of ice-movement in Ireland, indicated a northward trend from Connemara across Clew Bay ;

but the recognition of two epochs of ice-extension allow us to separate earlier from later deposits in this region, as we undoubtedly can on the eastern coast of Ireland. The local Connemara ice may have remained powerful, even when the continental type of ice-sheet prevailed in the plain. Its persistence from the earliest stage of the cold-epoch may have helped to direct the inland ice northward across the Ox Mountains from Castlebar to Killala Bay, a feature of the movement that was pointed out by Close. Undoubtedly ice from Connemara poured through the pass of Doolough north of Killary Harbour, right across the direction of the fjord, and it probably dammed up water to the east of it, as a lake in which the great drift-terraces of Leenane were laid down. It spread out over the lowlands towards Louisburgh, crossed Clew Bay, and left its detritus and signs of ice-plucking in the fine gap of Mallaranny between Curraun Achill and the central moors of Mayo. Achill itself was invaded by ice from the east, and boulder-drift, full of pebbles of Carboniferous limestone, forms cliffs on the west shore of the island.

The Connemara ice also spread eastward towards Lough Corrib, and southward across the Aran Islands, where it has left dark boulders of crystalline rock stranded, like the throwing-stones of giants, on the storm-swept limestone shelves. The surfaces of the Twelve Bens are magnificently smoothed by ice-action, and the lakelets beside the railway from Oughterard to Clifden often lie in glacial grooves.

Small terminal moraines, like those in the west of Clare Island, or the barriers in the Erriff Valley in Mayo and Glencar in Sligo, represent resting-stages in the melting of the latest glaciers. Out in the limestone plain eskers are common ; long, sinuous ridges of water-worn glacial drift, recording the choking of the channels

The Twelve Bens above Lough Inagh, Connemara
Glacial cirques in pre-Cambrian quartz

in which streams ran beneath a stagnating and continental type of ice-sheet.

Perched blocks, angular in form, and dropped on drift-deposits or on glaciated slabs of rock from the upper surface of the ice, are common throughout

Connaught. Some of the most interesting are those
consisting of limestone brought from the south-east,
which rest on the white gneiss of the Ox Mountain
range near Sligo.

The coast of Connaught, with its numerous sea-inlets
and outstanding isles, is clearly one of submergence.
Raised beaches, occurring in a few of the bay-heads,
indicate that the last movements have been upward;
but these have not balanced the subsidence that took
place after the western valleys had been carved by
streams. Evidence from southern Ireland shows that
this subsidence preceded the Glacial epoch. The glaciers
that moved soon afterwards down the inlets may have
pushed the sea-water before them, and may have ridden
over the islands, connecting them once more with the
land.

The great bay that extends from the south of
Co. Donegal to the north of Mayo possesses a synclinal
structure, and the downfold of the easily eroded limestone prepared the way for a lowland on which the sea
crept in easily. Clew Bay, as already noticed, has the
same structure; Galway Bay, however, with its granite
cut off straightly on the north and the high limestone
masses in Clare upon the south, seems to result from
subsidence along a line of fracture. Connemara thus
appears as a " horst," or upstanding mass of ancient
rocks, in regard to the submerged limestone on its
southern side. Killary Harbour, some 10 miles long
and in places only a quarter of a mile wide, is a genuine
fjord, and is aptly continued by the steep-sided Erriff
Valley at its head.

Maxwell Close urged that a general uplift of western
Ireland, reclaiming a broad territory from the Atlantic,

preceded the Glacial epoch and contributed to the
south-eastward flow of ice. The facts, however, of
Scandinavian glaciation, involving the formation of a
snow-dome in a comparative lowland, from which
glaciers reached the Atlantic across Norway and extended
to Dresden across the depression of the Baltic, render
a redistribution of land and water unnecessary in
accounting for ice-movements in Ireland. None the
less, after Glacial times, an uplift extended the country
westward, and peat and forests grew which are now
discovered only in dredgings off the coast. The submergence which gave us the present margin of Ireland
is thus of very recent origin, and a slight recovery is
possibly now in progress.

Loss of land by marine erosion is notable in the Aran
Islands and in the sculpturing of the great cliffs of
Achill. The limestone coast towards Sligo Bay suffers
from frequent undermining. Inland, the Corrib and
other rivers are carrying away tons of material daily
in solution from the limestone plain, where the acid
water from the bogs assists the process. The famous
dry canal near Cong, and numerous disappearing and
reappearing streams, illustrate the tendency of the
drainage to burrow underground.

The peat of the plains may still be flourishing, but
the conditions which covered the metamorphic hills of
Mayo with mountain-bog have probably already passed
away. Few parts of Ireland are so dreary as these
rounded moorlands, without crag or peak to break the
surface ; and the traveller's eye rests with relief upon
their Atlantic border, or on the woods planted along
the lakes that pass into the eastern plain.

The most important economic product connected with the geology of Connaught is the *coal* of the Lough Allen area. The seams occur high up on hilly outliers, and dip gently inwards in synclinal basins. Hence working is easy, and there is no speculation as to further concealed material. Interbedded shale has interfered with development east of the lake ; but a fair amount of bituminous coal is regularly extracted in the Arigna valley. Below the seams, which are in the Lower Coal Measures and Millstone Grit, numerous nodular bands of *clay ironstone* appear. These are of excellent quality and were formerly smelted at Creevelea ; but a considerable amount of covering rock must be removed for their development. *Iron ores* were also worked down to the eighteenth century, while the timber lasted for their smelting, in the Carboniferous country of Ballinrobe in Co. Mayo. *Copper pyrites* and *lead ore*, in the form of silver-bearing galena, occur in several places in the west of Co. Galway. Several mines were formerly worked near Oughterard.

Veins of *barytes* (barium sulphate) are mined on the plateau north of Glencar, on the Leitrim-Sligo border. The Carboniferous *limestone* of Galway and Roscommon forms an excellent building stone. Unfortunately, from its cheapness, it is used as the common *road-metal* in the plainlands. The comparative poverty of the districts to the west, where far better material freely occurs, prevents the use of steam-rolling, and the excellently graded roads of Connemara and southern Mayo are often surfaced too lightly for modern traffic, and fail to realise the intentions of their engineers. It may be mentioned that, with the exception of one or two places in the county of Donegal, no main routes

in the wilder parts of Ireland are so severely and reck-
lessly planned as those of Devonshire or northern
England. Moveover, the deep dissection of Connemara
and Mayo by streams and glaciers renders the passes
low, and improved metalling is all that is required
for the roads.

Co. Galway produces two well-known *marbles*, a
black Carboniferous variety at Menlo near Galway
town, and the unique serpentinous variety of Connemara. The latter is quarried on the prominent hill of
Lissoughter near Recess, and in the lowland farther
west at Ballynahinch and Streamstown. The influence
of intrusive rocks seems to be responsible for the
development of bands of olivine in this Pre-Cambrian
dolomitic limestone, an occurrence paralleled at Vesuvius
in the altered rocks of Monte Somma. The olivine is
now changed into serpentine, and the dark or light green
layers alternate very handsomely with white layers of
calcite. Occasionally a large knot of serpentine occurs ;
but the rock, which is.known as " Connemara green," is
essentially a limestone. It is quarried in considerable
blocks, and its value causes it to be sawn into thin slabs
for decoration.

Truly igneous serpentine (altered olivine-rock) occurs
as a sheet under Croaghpatrick and as dykes in Clare
Island and on the south side of Lough Gill. These
examples have not been used for ornamental purposes.

The *granite* which occurs in considerable variety in
the glaciated lowland on the north side of Galway Bay
is quarried at Shantallow near Galway, and should
repay further exploration from an ornamental point
of view. The Shantallow rock is a brown-red granite
of medium grain ; other types in Co. Galway display

red porphyritic felspars in a dark greenish micaceous ground.

The *soils* of Connaught are very various. On the limestone plain, grazing lands extend for hundreds of square miles ; little soil develops from the limestone itself, on account of its general purity. Near Sligo, however, the shaly type of deposit furnishes stiff lands.

Where the west winds sweep in full force across the limestone country, as in the Aran Islands and around Athenry, a soilless " karstland " is developed. The small amount of residue set free by the solution of the limestone is blown or washed away as quickly as it forms, and bare sheets of rock, with scanty vegetation hiding in its vertical joint-cracks, present a marked contrast with the pastures farther to the east. An equal contrast is seen as we cross the boundary between the plain and the Pre-Cambrian hills. Near Clew Bay, the carriage of limestone westward in the glaciers of the Ice-age has produced a certain amelioration ; but this has failed to influence the Old Red Sandstone fringe on the north side of the bay, which is little better than a desert. In the mountainous tracts of Mayo and Connemara, a few patches of boulder-drift, containing materials from various sources, are sufficient to attract the patient cultivator, while large areas of peaty land or of barren quartzite perforce remain untouched by tillage. The arable soils are often peaty, and in the limited plots that are available spade-labour is usually employed. Trees are greatly needed to protect the western farms. The action of proprietors in the sheltered valleys of Kylemore and Doolough in the Killary district has rendered these spots extremely beautiful, and the woodlands round Lough Gill send a

challenge even to Killarney. The destruction of forests
has, however, gone so far in the last three centuries that
it must be a long time before new plantations can cope
in the bare country of Belmullet or Achill Island with
the sweep of the Atlantic storms.

BOTANY

THE province of Connaught exhibits in the first place
a single broad contrast as regards its geology, and
consequently in its flora and fauna. Over the eastern
three-quarters of the area Carboniferous limestone
prevails, presenting in its characteristic form a low
undulating plain occupied mostly by grass-land and
peat bog. Over the remaining quarter, volcanic and
metamorphic rocks and ancient slates occupy the ground.
Heath, bog, and rock prevail everywhere ; much of the
ground is mountainous, with numerous lofty summits
looking down on lake-strewn barren lowlands. In
West Mayo 53 per cent. of the surface is occupied by
mountain and bog. Along the eastern boundary of
the province the River Shannon flows, a broad, slow
stream widening into island-studded lake-like expansions, with a remarkable flora and fauna. On the
western boundary of the limestone plain, where it abuts
on the metamorphic uplands, another string of lakes
is found, extending from Galway Bay to Killala Bay.
These also are of much interest to the naturalist. In
the north, in Sligo and Leitrim, the limestone rises into
a high table-land, dissected by deep valleys, and fringed
with magnificent cliffs. Here again an interesting flora

is found, of northern type, accompanied by some rare animals.

Along the western edge of the limestone plain drift and other coverings are often absent and the naked rock, seamed with innumerable fissures, the home of many rare plants, lies open to the sky. The transition from this limestone vegetation to that of the meta-morphic area immediately adjoining is extraordinarily abrupt and complete. All the characteristic plants of the limestone vanish at once, and in their place we get an ericaceous vegetation, which includes many of the peculiar southern and northern species for which the West of Ireland is famous. The corresponding change in the fauna has not yet been worked out in detail. The coast of Connaught is exceedingly broken and varied, offering every variety of habitat from huge precipices over 2000 ft. in height to wide sandy beaches and salt marshes ; but while some rare species occur, the maritime flora and fauna of the west coast is in general poorer than that of the east.

We can best obtain an idea of the flora by describing briefly certain chosen areas and mentioning their more interesting plants.

Connemara.—While this name is applied properly to that part of Co. Galway which lies west of Lough Corrib —the mountainous, metamorphic region—the botanist naturally groups with it the similar adjoining portion of Co. Mayo. This wild tract might well be known to him as the Land of the Three Heaths, from the out-standing feature of its vegetation—the occurrence there of three ericaceous plants, St Dabeoc's Heath (*Dabeocia polifolia*), the Mediterranean Heath (*Erica mediterranea*), and Mackay's Heath (*E. Mackaii*),

The Mediterranean Heath at Mallaranny

which are unknown elsewhere in the British Isles
or in Northern Europe, and are found only in S.W.
France and the Spanish Peninsula (except that
the first extends to the Azores). They constitute
one of the most striking groups in the "Lusitanian
flora" of Ireland, which, as pointed out in the
Ireland volume of the series, suggests an old continuous shore-line stretching north and south beyond
the present limits of Western Europe. Other
members of the southern group are also present
in Connemara—the London Pride, *Saxifraga umbrosa*
(abundant), Kidney-leaved Saxifrage, *S. Geum* (Clare
Island); the Irish Spurge, *Euphorbia hiberna* (Inishturk); the little Orchid, *Neotinia intacta*; and the
Maidenhair Fern, *Adiantum Capillus-Veneris*. Mixed
with these are many high northern types of European
or of American origin, such as *Dryas octopetala*, *Arctostaphylos Uva-ursi*, *Gentiana verna*, *Euphrasia Salisburgensis*, *Eriocaulon septangulare*, *Naias flexilis*. As
indicated elsewhere, the line of migration of some of
the southern species of the group is indicated by their
re-appearance in S.W. England, while a hint as to the
route of the northern elements is suggested by the fact
that a few of them still linger in the West of Scotland.
Osmunda regalis is everywhere. In the southern half
of Connemara the continuity of the bog flora, which
includes the three Droseras in abundance, *Utricularia
intermedia* and *U. ochroleuca*, *Rhynchospora fusca*,
Deschampsia discolor, etc., is broken only by patches
and fringes of cultivation, where the universal peat is
absent or has been cut away. In the northern half,
high rocky mountain-ranges rise (see next paragraph).
Along the eastern border, fringing Lough Corrib, a com-

Dryas octopetala and Neotinia intacta

pletely different flora is found where the peat-covered metamorphic rocks give way abruptly to bare limestones. The interesting flora of this region will be dealt with presently.

The Twelve Bens. — This beautiful mountain-group, formed mainly of quartzite, rises abruptly from the bog-covered plain of south Connemara to a height of nearly 2400 ft. On the east and north it is flanked by other ranges of almost equal elevation. The hills are extremely bare and rugged. Only a few of the characteristic Connemara plants mentioned in the preceding paragraph ascend the slopes, the southern *Saxifraga umbrosa*, which occurs equally at all elevations, and *Dabeocia polifolia*, being notable exceptions. The vegetation is scanty and poor, and interest centres in the colonies of alpine plants which occur here and there. Among these are *Thalictrum alpinum, Saxifraga oppositifolia, S. stellaris, Sedum Rhodiola, Saussurea alpina, Hieracium argenteum, Arctostaphylos Uva-ursi, Oxyria digyna, Salix herbacea, Juniperus nana, Carex rigida, Asplenium viride, Polystichum Lonchitis*. From the seaside *Silene maritima* and *Armeria maritima* come up to join these ; and among other uncommon species are *Meconopsis cambrica, Sagina subulata, Saxifraga grœnlandica, Crepis paludosa, Hymenophyllum unilaterale*.

Achill Island.—Achill will serve well as an example of the wind-swept, treeless, peat-covered areas that are characteristic of the extreme west. The island, which is separated from the mainland by a very narrow strait, is the most considerable on the Irish coast, having an area of 57 square miles. Not more than one-fifth of the surface is cultivated, or cultivable. The rest consists of undulating bogland, varied by several high ridges,

E

The Spring Gentian (*Gentiana verna*)

rising to about 2200 ft. The bogland is very poor in species, *Erica mediterranea* (confined to West Ireland and the Pyrenean region), being one of its few interesting plants. *Osmunda regalis* is abundant. Where the bog gets very wet, *Hypericum elodes, Drosera intermedia, Utricularia intermedia,* and *Carex limosa* become abundant, and *Lycopodium inundatum* occurs. In the numerous lakes we get *Ranunculus scoticus, Lobelia Dortmanna, Potamogeton filiformis,* the North American *Eriocaulon septangulare, Isoetes lacustris.* On the hills *Arctostaphylos Uva-ursi, Juniperus nana,* and the two Filmy Ferns are abundant, and higher up are several of the more widespread alpines, and also *Euphrasia foulaensis* in its only Irish station. The remarkable Liverwort flora of Slievemore is referred to later. The plants of the sea-cliffs include *Cochlearia grœnlandica, Sedum Rhodiola* (in abundance) and *Adiantum Capillus-Veneris.*

The Limestone Pavements.—As one travels westward across the great limestone plain of central Ireland, the covering of drift becomes thinner ; and near its western edge—roughly about the line of the railway which joins Ennis and Tuam—the drift is absent in patches, and the bare rock, deeply fissured owing to the action of rain and percolating water on the innumerable joints, stands out in knobbly flat sheets, grey and bare. The areas of bare rock increase in size and number as one approaches the edge of the limestone, until around the head of Galway Bay and fringing both sides of Lough Corrib we find miles of this curious surface. It attains its most striking development on the hills of the Burren district of Clare, south of Galway Bay (described in the *Munster* volume of this series), and its northern extension is continued as far as Lough Carra in Mayo. While at first glance these limestone pavements appear devoid of vegetation, closer examination reveals a rich flora nestling in the innumerable fissures. This flora is remarkable in its composition, including as it does a number of very rare plants, and vast quantities of others which are nowhere else in the country to be found in such profusion. The grey rocks are decked with the following plants, most of them occurring in very great abundance :—

Geranium sanguineum	Euphrasia Salisburgensis
Saxifraga hypnoides	Plantago maritima
Galium boreale	Spiranthes autumnalis
G. sylvestre	Neotinea intacta
Asperula cynanchica	Ophrys muscifera
Rubia peregrina	Sesleria cœrulea
Arctostaphylos Uva-ursi	Scolopendrium vulgare
Gentiana verna	Ceterach officinarum.

More locally we get *Viola stagnina, Rhamnus catharticus, R. Frangula, Spiræa Filipendula, Dryas octopetala, Cornus sanguinea, Juniperus nana, Taxus baccata,* and many other species. It will be observed at once what a curious assemblage of plants this is, embracing as it does a number of species of arctic and alpine distribution, such as the Dryas, Arctostaphylos, Gentiana and Sesleria, here growing at levels only a little above the sea, and with them southern forms, notably the Mediterranean *Neotinea intacta,* unknown elsewhere in northern Europe. Almost all these plants are here strictly limited to the areas of bare limestone, or to the esker ridges, formed entirely of limestone débris, that

The Pipewort (*Eriocaulon septangulare*), in Connemara

wind here and there over the plains, although a number of them are in other districts not confined to limestone rocks. It would seem that the physical as well as the chemical characters of these limestone areas affect the flora materially.

Lough Corrib and Lough Mask.—As already pointed out, these two lakes, which together extend for a distance of over 30 miles north and south, lie on the junction of the limestone, which stretches for 100 miles to the eastward, with the mountainous mass of metamorphic and igneous rocks which forms Connemara and West Mayo. As regards Lough Corrib, a narrow fringe of limestone, yielding the peculiar flora described in the last paragraph, extends along much of the western shore, but on Lough Mask the eastern side is formed of limestone, the western of older non-calcareous rocks, and the two shores present a striking contrast of floras, the one low, rocky, and much indented, with a grassy and bushy vegetation, the other stony and bare, rising, across a belt of poor cultivation, into heathery mountains. As regards the plants of the lakes themselves, *Ranunculus scoticus* and *Lobelia Dortmanna* grow on the shores of both. *Eriocaulon septangulare* occurs on Lough Corrib. Some very rare Pondweeds have their home here. The hybrid *P. Kirkii*, unknown elsewhere, grows in the river at Maam, and *P. Babingtonii* is only known from a specimen found floating loose in the lake in 1835. The northern *P. filiformis* is found in Lough Mask.

The Ben Bulben Plateau.—This area, lying north of Sligo town, presents a high moorland, 1000 to 2000 ft. in elevation, cut through by two deep and beautiful cliff-walled valleys, Glencar and Glenade, each em-

The Shrubby Cinquefoil (*Potentilla fruticosa*), at Ballyvaughan

bosoming a lake. Much of the periphery of the plateau
is likewise walled with lofty limestone cliffs. It is on
these cliff-ranges that the peculiar flora of the district
is developed, at an elevation of about 500 to 1500 ft.
Alpine plants are numerous, and often in great abundance—*Arenaria ciliata* (only station in the British Isles),
Saxifraga nivalis and *Epilobium alsinefolium* (only
station in Ireland), *Thalictrum alpinum, Draba incana,
Arabis petræa, Silene acaulis, Dryas octopetala, Saxifraga
aizoides, S. hypnoides, S. oppositifolia, Sedum Rhodiola*,
many *Hieracia, Vaccinium Vitis-Idæa, Polygonum vivi-
parum, Oxyria digyna, Salix herbacea, Juniperus nana,
Carex rigida, Sesleria cærulea, Poa alpina, Aspidium
Lonchitis, Asplenium viride*. Associated with these are
*Meconopsis cambrica, Polygala grandiflora, Vicia sylvatica,
Circæa alpina, Euphrasia Salisburgensis, Salix phylici-
folia. Adiantum Capillus-Veneris* grows in rock-chinks
high up on the cliffs, *Sisyrinchium augustifolium* in
sloping meadows below, and *Equisetum trachyodon* near
Glencar Lake. These lists convey an idea of the interesting nature of the flora, but the great grey rock-walls
clothed with alpine plants must be seen to be appreciated.

The River Shannon.—The upper reaches of the Shannon
lie within the province of Connaught ; and through all
the middle part of its course, from Roosky in Leitrim
to half-way down Lough Derg, it constitutes the eastern
boundary of that province. Throughout almost the whole
of its course it forms a broad, slow stream, with frequent
expansions and marshy shores. The two most notable
of its lakes—Lough Ree and Lough Derg—are dealt
with in other volumes of this series, the former under
Leinster, the latter under *Munster* ; and in the latter
volume a brief account is given of the botanical

Limestone Cliffs of Glencar, Co. Sligo, the Home of an Alpine Flora

characteristics of its wide estuary. In this place a few notes may be given of the more striking members of its flora. The reedy margins and adjoining ditches are the home of such species as *Ranunculus Lingua, Lathyrus palustris* (abundant in places), *Cicuta virosa* (north only), *Sium latifolium* (confined in Ireland to the basins of the Shannon and Erne), *Galium uliginosum, Hydrocharis Morsus-ranæ, Sagittaria sagittifolia.* Where the shores are hard, we find abundance of *Galium boreale* (in Ireland usually lowland), and *Teucrium Scordium* (unknown in the country outside the Shannon basin). *Inula salicina* is in the British Isles found only on stony ground around Lough Derg, on the limestone shores of which a very interesting flora is developed (described in the *Munster* volume). Below Lough Derg the Shannon drops rapidly to sea-level at Limerick. Where tidal muds begin the rare *Scirpus triqueter* appears in quantity—a plant unknown elsewhere in Ireland, and in Great Britain known only from three south of England estuaries. At Limerick it is associated with *Cochlearia anglica, Nasturtium sylvestre* and its allies, *Scirpus maritimus* and *S. Tabernaemontani.* Further down the estuary two very rare southern grasses are found—*Glyceria festucaeformis* and *G. Foucaudi.*

Some very rare species of mosses have been found in Connaught. Such are the southern *Tortula Vahliana* (known in Great Britain only from four vice-counties, and in Ireland from Leitrim and the Dublin district) ; *Trichostomum fragile* (in Sligo and West Galway ; also Kerry and Donegal : very rare and northern in Great Britain) ; *Zygodon gracilis* (West Galway and Yorkshire only) ; *Myurella julacea* (West Galway alone in Ireland ; very rare in Great Britain) ; *Ephemerum cohaerens*

(S.E. Galway only in Ireland : Sussex only (certainly) in England); and *Mnium riparium* (East Mayo, Armagh, and Antrim in Ireland : very rare in Great Britain). Other species which have their only Irish habitat in Connaught are *Dicranum uncinatum* (very fine on rocks on Nephin and Slievemore in Mayo) ; *D. montanum* (Slieve Gamph in Mayo) ; and *Eucalypta rhabdocarpa* and *Orthothecium rufescens* (both Sligo). The following species also deserve mention :—*Tortula princeps, Orthothecium intricatum*, and *Amblystegium confervoides* (all in Sligo) ; *Tortula gracilis* (East Mayo) ; *Hylocomium umbratum* (Slievemore, West Mayo) ; *Orthotrichum pallens* (N.E. Galway) ; *Ulota calvescens* (Leitrim and Sligo) ; and *Hypnum callichroum* (Leitrim).

The liverwort flora of Connaught resembles in a reduced measure that of Munster, being remarkable for certain species mainly of southern origin which occur in its western parts. Interest centres in the highlands and islands of Connemara and West Mayo, the great plain of limestone which extends to the eastward being nearly devoid of rare species, so far as is known. Perhaps the most remarkable plant which occurs is *Adelanthus dugortiensis* (Slievemore, Achill Island), a species unknown elsewhere, and having its nearest ally in the Southern Hemisphere. Other very rare plants are *Radula Holtii* (Bengorm and Old Head, West Mayo), and *Bazzania Pearsoni* (Slievemore, Achill Island) ; both are unknown in Great Britain. Among the species which find in Connaught their only Irish stations are *Radula Lindbergii* (Clare Island and Curraun Achill), *Prionolobus striatulus* (Clare Island), *Marsupella Jörgensenii*, and *M. Pearsonii* (both on Slievemore, Achill Island). Several other species, found elsewhere in Ireland (mostly in Kerry) but extremely rare in Great Britain, occur, such as *Radula Carringtonii* (Fermanagh, West Mayo, Kerry (frequent), Inverness); *R. voluta* (Kerry, Mayo, Cavan : very rare in Great Britain), *Mastigophora Woodsii* (Kerry, Achill Island, West Highlands), *Scapania nimbosa* (Brandon in Kerry, Slievemore in Mayo, Wales, West Highlands), *S. ornithopodioides* (Brandon in Kerry, Slievemore in Mayo, Wales, Cumberland, Scotland), *Gymnomitrium obtusum* (Down and West Mayo), *Pedinophyllum interruptum* (several counties), *Leptoscyphus cuneifolius* (Killarney, West Mayo, Scotland), and *Acrobolbus Wilsonii* (Cork, Kerry, West Mayo, West Inverness). The focus of rare Liverworts in Connaught, as will be seen from the above notes, is Slievemore on Achill (see p. 25). This fine hill, 2204 ft. in height, has a rocky scarp of mica-schist running up from base almost to summit, and facing west and north towards the ocean. It is these rocks which yield so remarkable a collection of scale-mosses, and some alpine flowering plants as well.

Of the Fungi, Lichens, and Algæ of Connaught it is impossible to speak within the compass of the present volume. It may be said, however, that the labours of lichenologists, notably of Larbalastier, have resulted in the finding of many notable species in Connemara, and that the Algæ of some of the large lakes and other areas have been well explored. The Fungi of Connaught were till recently quite unworked, but the recent survey of the Clare Island district has resulted in the publication of a list of over 800 species.

Croaghmore, Clare Island (1520 ft.), the home of many
Alpine plants

ZOOLOGY

TILL recently, the Red Deer (*Cervus elaphus*) still roamed over the mountains and moors of Connemara and Erris, but now Kerry is its only native stronghold. The Otter (*Lutra vulgaris*), Badger (*Meles taxus*), Fox (*Canis vulpes*), and Mountain Hare (*Lepus variabilis*) are frequent or common. The Pine Martin (*Mustela martes*) is seen occasionally. The most local of Irish Bats, the Lesser Horse-shoe (*Rhinolophus hipposideros*), has its headquarters in caves in Clare, whence it ranges into Galway and Kerry.

The Great Grey Seal (*Halichœrus grypus*) is abundant along the coast, being decidedly commoner than the Common Seal (*Phoca vitulina*). In 1895 the only known Irish specimen of the Ringed Seal (*Phoca fœtida*) was taken alive in Galway Bay, and lived for some years in the Dublin Zoo. This arctic species is extremely rare in the British Isles, there being only two other records (from Norfolk and Lincolnshire).

The inland parts of Connaught, presenting wide stretches of bog, marsh, and lake, have a large population of birds, affecting such habitats. In the more fertile parts woods are plentiful, providing ample cover for sylvan species. The wild and rocky coastal regions, with their treeless tracts of bog and mountain, huge cliffs, and numerous outlying islands, are the home of many cliff-haunting and shore-haunting species. The breeding birds of the lakes include the Shoveller, *Spatula clypeata*, and Tufted Duck, *Fuligula cristata* (both of which are increasing) ; the Red-breasted Merganser, *Mergus serrator* (often abundant) ; the Cormorant,

Phalacrocorax carbo (breeding in colonies in trees on islands, often among Herons ; also on old castles on islands) ; Common and Arctic Terns, *Sterna fluviatilis* and *S. macrura* ; several Gulls, *Larus ridibundus, L. canus, L. fuscus* ; and the Great Crested Grebe, *Podicipes cristatus*. Rarer breeders of the lakes are the Sandwich Tern, *Sterna cantiaca* ; and the Yellow Wagtail, *Motacilla Raii*, which in Ireland breeds only on Loughs Corrib, Mask, and Carra in Connaught, and Lough Neagh in Ulster.

On the bogs we get great colonies of Black-headed Gulls, *Larus ridibundus* ; and more rarely Lesser Black-backed Gulls, *L. fuscus*. The Marsh Harrier, *Circus æruginosus*, still breeds sparingly in spite of persecution ; and the Merlin, *Falco æsalon*, is not uncommon. On heaths the Stonechat, *Pratincola rubicola*, and Wheatear, *Saxicola œnanthe*, are everywhere abundant.

In the wooded and cultivated areas the more interesting breeding birds include the Whinchat, *Pratincola rubetra* (remarkably rare in Connaught) ; Blackcap, *Silvia atricapilla*, and Garden Warbler, *S. hortensis* (both local, the former increasing, the latter chiefly in the Shannon valley) ; Wood-Wren, *Phylloscopus sibilatrix* (rare) ; the Tree-creeper, *Certhia familiaris* (widespread) ; Siskin, *Carduelis spinus* (local) ; Golden-crested Wren, *Regulus cristatus* (common) ; Tree-Sparrow, *Passer montanus* (two colonies in Mayo —extremely local in Ireland) ; Crossbill, *Loxia curvirostra* (rare) ; Long-eared Owl, *Asio otus* (widespread) ; Heron, *Ardea cinerea* (frequent) ; and Woodcock, *Scolopax rusticula* (now an abundant breeder, having increased greatly in recent years).

Along the precipices which fringe the ocean in many places the Chough, *Pyrrhocorax graculus*, is abundant ; the Hooded Crow, *Corvus cornix*, is frequent ; and few cliff-ranges are without a pair of Ravens, *Corvus corax*, and Peregrines, *Falco peregrinus*. With them we get the Great and Lesser Black-backed Gulls, *Larus marinus* and *L. fuscus* ; while the lower parts of the cliffs are often tenanted by vast numbers of Guillemots, *Uria troile* ; Razorbills, *Alca torda* ; Puffins, *Fratercula arctica* ; Herring Gulls, *Larus argentatus* ; Kittiwakes, *Rissa tridactyla* ; Shags, *Phalacrocorax graculus* ; and Cormorants, *P. carbo*. In more remote spots, especially on the islands, a considerable number of Manx Shear-waters, *Puffinus anglorum*, and Stormy Petrels, *Procellaria pelagica*, are known to breed, and also, sparingly, Leach's Fork-tailed Petrel, *Oceanodroma leucorhoa*. An interesting recent addition to the list of Irish breeding birds is the Fulmar, *Fulmarus glacialis*, lately found on the huge cliffs of North Mayo and on an adjoining island, and also in Donegal and Kerry, and still increasing. On the lower parts of the coast the most interesting inhabitant is the Red-necked Phalarope, *P. hyperboreus*, which breeds on a large lonely salt-marsh facing the Atlantic.

On the mountains the Curlew, *Numenius arquata*, and the Golden Plover, *Charadrius pluvialis*, inhabit the high moors and bring out their young.

Along the rivers the Kingfisher, *Alcedo ispida* ; the Dipper, *Cinclus aquaticus* (Irish form) ; and the Grey Wagtail, *Motacilla melanope*, are frequent and characteristic.

As in other Irish districts, we have records of certain striking changes in the bird population ; some species have arrived or increased, others diminished. The Magpie, *Pica rustica*, first seen in Ireland in the seventeenth century, has spread to the remotest corners of the west. The same applies to the Mistle-Thrush, *Turdus viscivorus*, which only reached this country at the beginning of the nineteenth century. The Stock-Dove, *Columba œnas*, is another recent arrival. The Starling, *Sturnus vulgaris*, formerly rare, is now found in the remotest parts of the province. The Jackdaw, *Corvus monedula*, another increasing species, is still absent from most of the western islands, where its place is taken by the Chough, *Pyrrhocorax graculus*. The Woodcock, *Scolopax rusticula* ; Shoveller, *Spatula clypeata* ; and Tufted Duck, *Fuligula cristata*, have also greatly increased their breeding range.

Of birds which have decreased in the district, the most interesting are the Golden Eagle, *Aquila chrysaëtus*, which bred till a few years ago, and of which a single specimen haunted the cliffs of Mayo till it was shot quite lately ; and the White-tailed Eagle, *Haliaëtus albicilla*, which till recently bred in many places, but is now on the point of extinction. The Quail, *Coturnix comnunis*, formerly abundant, is now almost unknown.

As regards winter visitors, a very rare species, which has occurred chiefly in Western Connaught, is the Mealy Redpoll, *Linota linaria*. Those two rare and handsome northern winter visitors, the Greenland Falcon, *F. candicans*, and the Snowy Owl, *Nyctea scandiaca*, have occurred more frequently in Mayo than in any other Irish county. The Glaucous and Iceland Gulls, *Larus glaucus* and *L. leucopterus*, are among the occasional winter visitors. The stay of the Snow Bunting, *Plecto-*

F

phenax nivalis, is remarkably prolonged in Connaught, specimens occurring as late as the end of May.

As elsewhere in Ireland, the winter avifauna is increased by the immigration from the east of great flocks of Redwings, *Turdus iliacus*; Fieldfares, *T. pilaris*; Song Thrushes, *T. musicus*; Blackbirds, *T. merula*; Skylarks, *Alauda arvensis*; Meadow Pipits, *Anthus pratensis*; and Chaffinches, *Fringilla cœlebs*. The regular winter visitors include vast numbers of ducks, geese, and swans of many species, which frequent the bays and lakes.

The only known Irish examples of the Short-toed Lark, *Alauda brachydactyla*; Lesser Golden Plover, *Charadrius dominicus*; American Pectoral Sandpiper, *Tringa maculata*; and Greater Snow-Goose, *Chen nivalis* (only European occurrence of this Greenland bird), have been obtained in Connaught. A Red-throated Pipit, *Anthus cervinus*, from Achill Island, is also the only Irish specimen.

The leading features of the avifauna of the islands of West Mayo, the portion of the west coast of Ireland which has been most closely studied, are thus summarised by R. J. Ussher :[1]

1. Resident land-birds are of few species, including the Stonechat, Hedgesparrow, Dipper, Wren, Twite, three Buntings, and the more characteristic Rock Pipit, Chough, Raven, Peregrine, and Rock-Dove, and formerly the Golden Eagle.

2. Summer land-birds that breed are still fewer : the Wheatear, Whitethroat, Sedge-Warbler, Swallow, Cuckoo, Corn-crake.

[1] Clare Island Survey, part 20, Aves. *Proc. Roy. Irish Academy*, Vol. xxxi., 1912.

3. There are colonies of Shags, cliff-breeding Gulls, Arctic and Little Terns, Auks and Petrels, and many Oyster-catchers nest.

The more special features are :

4. The large immigration of passerine birds that resort to the islands and the Mullet in winter for a milder climate, as do the Thrush family, Finches, Starlings, Rooks, and Skylarks.

5. The winter visitation of species from northern countries, which resort to the western fringe of Ireland, especially the north-west, *e.g.*, the Snow Bunting, Greenland Falcon, Wild Swans, and Arctic species of Gulls.

6. The late stay in spring of the above winter birds and such others as the Scaup Duck, Sanderling, Purple Sandpiper, Northern Diver, and Sclavonian Grebe.

7. The stay throughout the summer of adolescent winter visitors, as the Turnstone, Bar-tailed Godwit.

8. The rarity or absence of those occasional visitors that come from the Continent, as the Black Redstart, the rarer Herons and Crakes.

9. The increase of the Blackbird and of several woodland species on the mainland, and of the Great Black-backed Gull on the islands.

The only Irish Reptile, the Viviparous Lizard (*Lacerta vivipara*) is frequent here as elsewhere, and occurs on some of the islands lying off the coast. The Common Frog (*Rana temporaria*) and Common Newt (*Molge vulgaris*), though common on the mainland, do not occur on the outlying islands.

Of the Salmonidæ, the Salmon *S. salar* ; Sea Trout, *S. trutta* ; and Brown Trout, *S. fario*, in its various forms, are abundant ; many of the western Salmon fisheries are very valuable. Of the puzzling group of the Chars, *Salvelina Colei* occurs in lakes in Galway and Mayo. An interesting fish is the endemic Shannon Pollan, *Coregonus elegans* ; the group to which it belongs has its headquarters in Lough Neagh in Ulster, but this form occurs only in the Shannon lakes. The two Shads, *Clupea finta* and *C. alosa*, are occasionally taken, and most of the smaller species which go to make up the rather limited Irish fish fauna also occur in the province.

Although Connaught is in most groups a centre for the peculiar southern fauna which renders Ireland so interesting a country to the naturalist, this does not apply to the snails. The molluscan fauna is large and varied, but does not include any species of such special interest as the Geomalacus of Munster. There is a broad contrast in geology and scenery in the province, between mountainous metamorphic areas and plains (sometimes hills) of limestone ; but in both types of country there is a full molluscan fauna. In the metamorphic area, the district around Ballynahinch and Roundstone in Connemara, for instance, can be specially recommended to the conchologist ; while on the limestone area, the woods and glens in the Sligo district supply magnificent collecting ground. Among the rarer or more interesting species are : *Zonitoides excavatus* (Galway and Mayo), *Helicella barbara* (widespread, occurring both on the coast and inland), *Hygromia granulata* (Ballina estuary, Co. Sligo), *Acanthinula lamellata* (in all native woodlands), *Arianta arbustorum* (Sligo and Leitrim—in Ireland confined to the N. and N.W.), *Cæcilioides acicula* (Clare and Galway),

Dog's Bay (Port-na-fedog), Connemara

Pupa anglica (widespread), *Vertigo Lilljeborgi* (shores of Ballynahinch Lake, Connemara, and Glenade Lough, Co. Leitrim ; elsewhere in Ireland known only from Lough Allua in Cork), *Succinea oblonga* (abundant at Dooaghtry in West Mayo), *Bithynia Leachi* (Grand Canal, South Galway ; extremely local in Ireland), *Acicula lineata* (in all the coastal districts), *Margaritana margaritifera* (local), *Pisidium Lilljeborgi* (Achill Island, West Mayo ; elsewhere in Ireland known only from Kerry, Westmeath, Fermanagh, Antrim, and Donegal), *P. hibernicum* (Kerry, Galway, Sweden).

One of the most remarkable features in connection with the entomology of Connaught as at present known is the number of rare Lepidoptera which have rewarded the careful collecting of Lord Clonbrock at Clonbrock, in the north-eastern part of Co. Galway. This locality is flat and open, with a good deal of wood and bog. Here have been taken the only Irish specimens of *Lycæna astrarche* (var. *artaxerxes*), and of the following moths : *Spilosoma urticæ, Hepianus sylvanus, Heterogenea limacodes, Ptilophora plumigera, Dipterygia scabriuscula*, the northern *Pachnobia hyperborea* (var. *carnica*), *Cerastis erythrocephala, Oporina croceago, Xanthia gilvago*, and *Cucullia lychnitis*. A few other species, which have occurred in the adjoining parts of Galway, are also unknown elsewhere in Ireland : *Argynnis adippe, Callegenia miniata, Moma orion* (Clonbrock and Mote Park, the latter locality lying 20 miles N.N.E. of the former, in Co. Rescommon), *Leucania turca, Hadena rectilinea*, and *Calocampa solidaginis*. Other rare Clonbrock species, which have, however, additional stations in Ireland, are *Drepana falcula, Thecla betulæ, Smerinthus tiliæ, Stauropus jagi, Notodonta chaonia, Leucania impudens, Xanthia citrago, X. aurago, Hecatera chryso-zona,* and *Pericallia syringaria.*

Reference may also be made to the following rare Connaught insects : among the Butterflies, *Gonepteryx rhamni,* so local in Ireland, is frequent in Co. Galway, where its food-plant, the Buckthorn—also local in the country—occurs in many places ; and the rare alpine *Erebia epiphron* (var. *cassiope*) has been taken on Croagh-patrick and Nephin in Mayo. Among the Moths, the

The Galway Burnet-moth

Galway Burnet, *Zygæna pilosellæ,* var. *nubigena,* belongs essentially to this district, occurring in Ireland only on the limestone pastures around Galway Bay ; *Dicranura bifida* has been taken at Markree in Sligo, and *Cucullia chamomillæ* at Kilcornan (Co. Galway) and in Sligo. A specimen of the rare *Dasydia obfuscaria* was recently obtained on Clare Island in Co. Mayo. In many places on the sandhills of the coast *Nyssia zonaria* may be found.

Among the beetles some rare species occur. On the mountains we get *Carabus glabratus* (Ben Bulben), *Cymindis vaporariorum* (Achill and Croaghpatrick), and

Leistus montanus (mountain summits in Mayo and Galway). The fauna has a distinctly northern facies, as shown by the presence of such species as *Pelophila borealis* (Galway, Mayo, Roscommon, Sligo), *Blethisa multipunctata* (Galway, Roscommon, Sligo), *Agabus congener* (lakes on Mweelrea, Mayo, only Irish station), *Silpha dispar* (Galway and Roscommon), *Donacia obscura* (Moycullen, Co. Galway), *Otiorrhynchus blandus* (Galway, Mayo, Sligo), and *Erirrhinus æthiops* (Galway and Roscommon). Against these we have very few species of southern type, but *Cetonia aurata*, which occurs at Roundstone in Galway, and is abundant a few miles further south on the Aran Islands (just outside our district) is a case in point. Two species taken in Cloonca Wood, Roscommon, have not been found elsewhere in Ireland : *Hylotrupes bajulus* and *Lytta vesicatoria*. *Aepus Robinii* has been found between tide-marks in the Clare Island district in Mayo ; *Panagæus crux-major*, on the shores of Castlebar Lough ; *Carabus clathratus*, on bogs in Galway, Mayo, and Sligo. The endemic *Silpha subrotundata* is abundant in the province, as elsewhere in Ireland ; and *Rhopalomesites Tardyi*, so rare outside Ireland, is noted from both Mayo and Galway, and is probably frequent. The local Musk Beetle, *Aromia moschata*, has been taken at Clonbrock in Galway ; *Lema septentrionalis* is also on record from Galway, and *Bembidium quadripunctatum* from Portumna on the Shannon.

Two of the most interesting Spiders of the district are *Theonoe minutissima* and *Pardosa purbeckensis*, neither of which has so far been found outside the British Isles. Both have been taken in Co. Galway, and the first occurs also in Ulster, the second also in

Munster. The following have their only Irish station within the present district, and are rarities also in England : *Pedanostethus arundinetus* (Galway and Mayo), *Cornicularia vigilax* (Galway), *Tetragnatha nigrita* (Roscommon), *Eugnatha striata* (Sligo), *Suiga sanguinea* (Galway). The local Spiders also include the northern *Xysticus sabulosus* (Galway and Roscommon), *Metopobactrus prominulus* (Mayo), *Euophrys petrensis* (Galway), *Peponocranium ludicrum, Hilaira excisa, H. uncata*, and *Diplocephalus castaneipes* (all from Mayo), *Diplocephalus Beckii* (Sligo), and *Attus floricola* (Galway). *Tegenaria hibernica* has been taken at Woodford in Galway. This grand species, unknown outside Ireland, has its headquarters in Co. Dublin, occurring also in Wicklow and Cork. Its nearest relative is found in the Pyrenees, and it is to be regarded as a member of the old Lusitanian group of animals which are now found mainly in the Pyrenees and the West of Ireland, occurring also sparingly in south-western England ; and which are held by most authorities to indicate the existence in long bygone times of a continuous western European shore-line, probably far to the westward of the present Continental edge. The following noteworthy species are widely distributed in Ireland : *Cyclosa conica, Pisaura mirabilis, Misumena vatia* and *Angelina labyrinthica* (all occurring in Co. Galway) ; and *Dolomedes fimbriatus* (frequent in Connaught).

In conclusion, reference may be made to one or two species belonging to other groups of animals, which are especially interesting on account of their distribution, since consideration of space preclude any more full account. The rare Dragonfly, *Ischnura pumilio*, occurs in Galway and Mayo, and the Caddisfly, *Limnophilus fuscinerviis,* found on the margins of Castlebar Lough, has not been taken elsewhere in the British Isles. *Aepophilus Bonnairei* is a rare hemipteron which is recorded from Galway Bay and Blacksod Bay, where it lives between tide-marks. It is a member of the Lusitanian fauna, being restricted elsewhere to S.W. England, France, and Spain. The large Grasshopper, *Mecostethus grossus,* is not uncommon in Mayo and Galway; it is an insect of puzzling distribution, being distinctly northern except in the British Isles, where it inhabits the Fen country in England and the west and south of Ireland, and occurs also in the Channel Islands. The fresh-water sponge, *Heteromeyenia Ryderi,* known only from North America, Ireland, and Scotland, is abundant in lakes except where limestone is present.

ANTIQUITIES

THERE appear to have been a number of Neolithic settlements throughout the province of Connaught. In the Bronze Age the civilisation, as attested by the various ornaments of gold and weapons of bronze that have been found, appears to have been of an advanced character. When we come to the period embraced by the Irish Heroic tales Connaught figures largely in connection with the famous Queen Meadhbh, whose palace was at Rathcroghan, Co. Roscommon. In Christian times, we find in Co. Mayo the mountain of Croaghpatrick, where St Patrick retired for prayer and fasting, and which has since become a place of pilgrimage for the whole Irish nation. Many of the cathedrals and other churches claim to have been founded by

Ireland's apostle during his sojourn in Connaught. The two best-known antiquities of the Christian period associated with the province are the *Fiacail Phádraig* (Shrine of St Patrick's Tooth), and the Cross of Cong, both of which are now preserved in the National Museum, Dublin.

It has been necessary to treat the various antiquities and architectural remains with regard to the space at the writer's command, and with a view to giving a general idea of the archæological features of the province : many interesting monuments have had to be left undescribed, others are merely mentioned. It is, however, hoped that the account may convey some idea of the antiquities to be seen in this portion of Ireland.

The dolmens of Connaught number, according to Borlase,[1] 248, this being the largest total for any province of Ireland. Sligo heads the list with 163, Mayo possesses 45 dolmens, and Galway 30, while there are 6 in Roscommon and 4 in Leitrim. Owing to limits of space only the megalithic monuments of Sligo, which exceed in interest those of the other counties, will be described in detail.

The most remarkable of the Sligo monuments is the structure situated in the Deerpark. It has been compared to Stonehenge on account of the trilithons which occur in both monuments, but the Irish structure is on such a much smaller scale, that no comparison between the two is really permissible. The monument is situated on a hill, some 500 ft. above sea-level, about 4 miles east of the town of Sligo. It consists of a central enclosure about 50 ft. long, having at the

[1] *The Dolmens of Ireland*, 1897, Vol. ii., p. 418.

west end a long cist divided in the middle into two compartments, and, at the east, two long cists with a passage between them, each being divided into two. At the eastern end the openings into the cists are composed of trilithons : there is another at the opening into the cist at the west end. The cists at each end were originally covered with roofing slabs : they were places of burial, human bones having been discovered in them.

Next in importance to the monument in the Deerpark is the great carn situated on the summit of Knocknarea mountain, traditionally reputed to be the burial place of Queen Meadhbh. The carn is a vast pile of stones about 590 ft. in circumference, and nearly 35 ft. in height. On a clear day a splendid view of the district can be obtained from this carn : as it is conspicuous from all parts of the surrounding country, it would appear to have been the burial place of some person of importance. Some smaller ruined carns and megalithic monuments to be seen at the foot of the great carn possibly contained the bodies of dependents, or slaves, of the occupant of the principal monument.

Three miles south-west of the town of Sligo, are the series of megalithic remains generally known as the " Carrowmore Cromlechs." This group of monuments is situated on a raised table-land, extending about a mile in one direction, and half a mile in the other. The antiquities are of various descriptions : dolmens, surrounded with stone circles ; carns ; cists ; and stone circles. The finest dolmen of the group, locally known as the bed of the warriors, is situated on the ridge of a hill ; it is surrounded by a stone circle. Seven feet in height, it is practically perfect, with a remarkable porch-like entrance. The monuments are supposed to

A Dolmen at Carrowmore, Co. Sligo

mark the site of the battle of Northern Moytura. Excavations, unfortunately of an unscientific character, have been undertaken from time to time in many of the dolmens and cists ; some of the objects found are now preserved in the National Museum, Dublin. The remains discovered include calcined human bones, burial urns, steatite beads, some flint flakes, etc. There can be no doubt that the monuments were sepulchral. Another tomb which is often considered to form part of the Carrowmore group, is a grave at Cloverhill in the neighbourhood of the Carrowmore monuments. The grave, which appears to be of Bronze-Age date, is horseshoe-shaped ; it measures 5 ft. 9 ins. in length, and 3 ft. 6 ins. across at the widest part : it is formed of large stones, some of which are incised with centered circles and spiral designs.

Another series of monuments in Co. Sligo is a group of fourteen burial carns, two ruined dolmen-like structures, and the remains of an ancient village settlement. All these antiquities are situated on Carrowkeel mountain overlooking Loch Arrow. Carrowkeel is a flat-topped hill of wide extent, with a maximum elevation of 1029 ft. The group of prehistoric buildings was excavated in 1911 with interesting archæological results. Most of the carns proved to contain cruciform chambers with roofs formed by false doming similar to, only smaller than, the chambers at New Grange, Co. Meath. The most interesting carn of the series consisted of two chambers, separated by a narrow doorway, with three grave recesses in the inner chamber and two in the outer. In the inner chamber was a standing stone 5 ft. high, apparently a religious emblem, so that this carn seems to have been a temple as well as a place of burial. It was 87 ft. in diameter and about 25 ft. high. The remains discovered in the carns consisted of burnt and unburnt human bones, stone beads, Bronze-Age pottery, and bone implements. A large number of individuals had been buried, and the interments had probably lasted over a considerable time. The remains of the village are on a bare rocky platform : enough of the structures remain to show the details. They consist of two rings of upright slabs with small stone fillings between them, the walls being about 3 ft. thick. Forty-seven of these rings can be distinguished ; the enclosures were probably protecting walls, within which dwellings of some temporary nature, such as huts or tents, were erected. It is possible that this settlement was occupied by the builders of the carns, if so, it must be considered as one of the oldest known village sites in Northern Europe.

There are some 7593 forts of various kinds marked on the ordnance maps for the province of Connaught. Many of these, built of stone, are of large proportions; others are promontory forts, others again, earthen rings. Some may be definitely considered as Norman motes, bearing witness to the Norman occupation of Connaught. Excepting the Norman motes, it is difficult to arrive at any definite dates for the building and occupation of the remaining forts ; some probably go back to the Bronze Age or even to the Neolithic period, but many of the smaller earthen ring forts are probably the remains of moated homesteads of mediæval days ; others are probably cattle pens, with the walls built solid to keep out wolves.

The most striking of all the Irish forts is the

group in the north island of Aran, off the coast of
Galway. They comprise the great forts of *Dún Aonghusa*, *Dún Eoghanacht*, *Dún Eochla*, *Dubh Chathair*,
four defaced cahers near *Dún Eochla*, and other remains. *Dún Aonghusa*, the largest of these, has probably appealed to the imagination of antiquaries more
than any other Irish fort. It is perched on the summit
of a hill, on the edge of a precipitous sea-cliff about
300 ft. high. According to legend, the fort was built
by the sons of Ughmhór, a Fir Bolg tribe, who, being
oppressed by the king of Tara, left their settlements
in Meath and fled to the west. They were befriended
by Queen Meadhbh, and settled around Clew Bay and
Galway Bay about the first century of the Christian
era. *Dún Aonghusa* was according to tradition founded
by *Aongus*, son or descendant of Ughmhór ; it is considered to have originally consisted of three oval rings
which have been cut into by the sea for about half
their extent. It is possible that this was the case,
but it may have always belonged to the crescent type
common among promontory forts. It now consists of
four walls, and Mr T. J. Westropp,[1] in his study of this
fort, suggests that it probably consisted originally of a
simple oval ring wall, which was next strengthened
by a second ring nearly equi-distant from the first, a
third wall being added later, and an elaborate abattis
of close-set pillar stones set round this. Lastly, a large
irregular space was enclosed by another wall, defending
the approach from the landing-place at Port Murvey.
The inner fort is 150 ft. in diameter, the rampart has
a slight batter, and is 12 ft. to 13 ft. high. The well
preserved gateway is composed of a long outer lintel

[1] *Proceedings of the Royal Irish Academy*, Vol. xxviii., Sec. C, p. 1.

with two long relieving stones over it.   It is 5 ft. 9 ins.

Dún Aonghusa

high, but an inside step of natural rock lowers it to
5 ft. 3 ins.   The middle wall varies from about 5 ft. to

G

12 ft. in height, it is terraced throughout. The north
gate is 4 ft. 3 ins. high. The enclosure is now about
400 ft. east and west, by 200 ft. north and south. The
abattis, one of the most remarkable features of this
fort, consists of a closely-set mass of little pillars,
usually 3 ft. or 4 ft. high, which gird the whole of the
middle walls in a band from 30 ft. to 80 ft. wide. They
measure about 700 ft. from the west to the north-east
gate, and over 200 ft. from it to the cliff eastward.
The tops of the pillars are much weathered, but they
are difficult to pass even undefended. They were
compared by O'Donovan to an army petrified in the
act of attack. The much-levelled outer rampart is
spread from about 10 ft. to 15 ft. wide : where it is well
preserved it shows two faces of carefully laid blocks.
The wall is over 2000 ft. in length ; its girth is 1250 ft.
by the cliff edge, 1174 ft. across from east to west ; and
650 ft. deep past the eastern face of the abattis north
and south. There is, on the north side of this wall,
a nearly perfect gateway of similar type to the others
already mentioned. It is difficult to estimate the age
of this great fort in which worked implements of flint,
and chert, and also some bronze ornaments, have been
found. It was restored in 1884, and, in the opinion of
experts, the restoration, having been of too thorough
a character, has complicated any estimation as to the
date of the original building.

Of the other forts of this group we may mention
Dubh Chathair, Aranmore, which consists of a dry-stone
wall 220 ft. long, 20 ft. high, and 15 ft. to 18 ft. thick,
built across a long headland. The fort was protected
on the land side by an abattis. Inside the wall were
two rows of stone huts. *Dún Chonchobhair*, Inishmaan

(middle island), on the middle island of Aran, is a remarkable structure ; it occupies a commanding position overlooking the whole island, being visible from the mainland of Clare and Galway. It is a long oval fortification on the edge of a low ridge ; it measures internally 227 ft. north and south, and 115 ft. east and west. The gateway is defaced. The wall was terraced and had flights of steps. A group of huts was situated at the northern end. The fort has suffered from injudicious restoration.

Rathcroghan, near Ballanagare, Co. Roscommon, is the most romantic earthwork in Connaught. The mound has borne the name of *Raith Cruachain* from early times ; it is a flat-topped oval, nearly circular, about 98 yards in diameter at the base, and about 68 yards across the top, which is only about 12 ft. above the surrounding ground level. About 800 yards south of the mound is a curious enclosure containing the remains of huts, which is known as the *Roilig na Riogh* (Cemetery of the Kings) and close to this is a small ring enclosing a pillar stone, known as the pillar stone of Dathi, who was the last pagan king of Ireland. Rathcroghan has been identified with the palace of the kings of Connaught and especially with Queen Meadhbh, the heroine of the early Irish tale, the *Táin Bó Cuailgne*. Rathcroghan is only one of the numerous mounds which cover the whole surrounding plain ; it is possible that it may be sepulchral, and that the name *Roilig na Riogh* applies to the tumuli as a whole rather than to the curious ring which now bears that name. Careful excavation of a number of the tumuli is needed to give any certainty in the matter ; a recent excavation of the

Roilig na Riogh did not bring to light either human or artificial remains.

Another interesting monument is *Carn Fraoich* (Carnfree), the inauguration mound of the O'Conors. Situated about 3 miles to the south-east of Rathcroghan, it now consists of a small carn of earth and stones about 41 ft. in circumference and 8 ft. in height. It is situated on a lofty eminence, and from it may be seen one of the finest views of pastoral country in Ireland. As has been said by Sir William Wilde, " A grander spot, or a more enchanting view, could not be obtained by a King of Ireland as he stood on the inauguration Carn, with his face to the north, his feet on the Sacred Stone, and amidst the shouts of thousands was handed the white wand of Sovereignty."

In the field adjoining the inauguration mound is a conical earthen tumulus, some 20 ft. high and 81 paces in girth, surrounded by a fosse and earthen ring. Near the tumulus stands a ring fort, enclosing a pillar stone 10 ft. high, not improbably the inauguration pillar of Carnfree.

Among the fortifications of the province may be mentioned the promontory forts on the coast of Mayo. They have been scientifically examined by Mr T. J. Westropp, who has published his account of them in the *Journal of the Royal Society of Antiquaries of Ireland*, 1912. He considers that the bulk of these forts could only have been suitable as places of refuge for the inhabitants of the islands and coasts during sudden raids, they stand on the high headlands of a coast lacking harbours, consequently they cannot have been of use to an invading force. It is impossible to give any general description of these forts, as many of them are of divergent types, their plans must be studied in Mr Westropp's account. It may however be stated that the dating of such structures is extremely difficult; without scientific excavation it is impossible to say to how early, or to how late, a date their occupation may have extended.

The Lough Hackett group of forts in Co. Galway is important. It covers a district of 7 miles by 14 miles in extent to the north-east of Lough Corrib. Ninety-one forts and numerous other remains are included in this

Prehistoric Stone Fort at Caherweelder, Co. Galway

group. Many of the forts are built of stone, and contain souterrains. Another large group in Co. Galway is situated in a district lying at the eastern end of Galway Bay from Oranmore to Craughwell and southward to Ardrahan and Finvarra, about 10 miles by 7 miles in extent. There are over fifty forts in this group, as well as other antiquities. *Cahergeal* in the first of these groups, a large stone fort situated about 2 miles from Lough Corrib, is probably the best known as it was described by Sir William Wilde in his book on Lough Corrib. It is a large ring fort having an internal diameter of 117 ft. The wall being some 7½ ft. to 9 ft. 4 ins. thick, and formerly from 16 ft. to 20 ft. high. There are steps made of large projecting blocks like those of a modern stile in the wall, and a gateway facing south-east with jamb-stones 5 ft. 8 ins. high.

A large circular earthen ring at Masonbrook, near Loughrea, Co. Galway, contains within the ring a circle of seven stones each 4 ft. or 5 ft. in height: in the centre is a low mound capped by a pile of stones. Recent excavation beneath the mound did not result in the discovery of human or artificial remains, leading to the supposition that the ring was used for the celebration of religious rites, not as a place of interment.

Colonel Wood-Martin (*Lake Dwellings of Ireland*, 1886) published a map showing the approximate distribution of the Irish lake-dwellings; according to this there are seventy-one recorded crannogs for the province of Connaught, but the total number is probably considerably greater.

Of these Ardakillen Crannog was explored in a satisfactory manner, and from it a number of objects of importance, most of which are now in the National Museum, Dublin, were obtained. The crannog, constructed both of stones and oak piling, was one of four which were discovered when the level of the lake was lowered. A deep layer of loose stones was bounded by an enclosing wall, the foundation being supported by piling, over the stones was a slight deposit of earth. The lower portion of the island consisted of clay, peat, and stones mingled with ashes, bones, and timber logs. A large quantity of bones and a number of interesting objects were discovered on the island. A canoe was found close to the crannog, 40 ft. in length, it was made from a single oak tree ; in it were found a skull, a spear-head, and a bronze pin. The skull shows the marks of a great number of cuts, due apparently to blows with a sword received during life. A neckpiece of iron with a piece of iron chain attached to it was found near the skull. The antiquities discovered included a beautiful bronze hinge-brooch decorated with La Tène C-curves and plait work ; this, known as the " Ardakillen " brooch, has frequently been described and illustrated ; a large number of pins of bone, twenty-two combs, the bronze cheek-piece of a horse's bit, a bronze rapier-blade, glass and amber beads, numerous pins of bronze, hair-pins, and other objects.

The island of Inismurray, Co. Sligo, which lies 4 miles from the coast of Sligo, at the entrance of Donegal Bay, contains some early ecclesiastical antiquities of considerable interest. The archæological remains include churches, cells, underground passages, *leacs*, tombs, inscribed stones, and one of the most perfect cashels in Ireland. Lord Dunraven, when speaking of the island in his *Notes on Irish Architecture*, said: "the group of ruins here offer the most characteristic example now in existence of the earliest monastic establishments in Ireland." The island is associated with St Molaise, who lived in the sixth century. The cashel, which is 175 ft. long and 135 ft. broad, is built of dry stones. The walls vary from about 7½ ft. to 9¾ ft. in height ; they contain several passages and small chambers. Three bee-hive cells are situated within the enclosure, including the so-called " school-house," an oval building constructed of large stones, and the *Tráth an Chorghais* or Lent Station. Within the cashel are three small churches called *Teach Molaise*, *Teampull na bfear* (the church of the men), and *Teampull na Teineadh* (the church of the fire). Outside the cashel is a small oratory called *Teampull na mban* (the church of the women). Inside the cashel are three altars, and many more are to be seen on the island. Several early grave slabs with Irish inscriptions, and some pillar stones may also be noticed.

Clare Island : Mr T. J. Westropp has described this, and the other islands of the same group, in his paper on the History and Archæology of the locality printed in the Royal Irish Academy's survey of Clare Island.

Clare Island (*Cliara*) is situated in Clew Bay off the coast of Mayo ; it is not rich in prehistoric monuments : a bronze spear has been found there, but no other portable antiquities have up to the present been recorded as discovered in the island. It contains a pillar stone ; what appears to be a small stone circle ; and six cliff or promontory forts. The principal antiquity on the island is the small monastic church ; the monastery of which it formed part was a Carmelite cell, dedicated to the Virgin, which was afterwards attached to the Cistercian House of Knockmoy ; it was founded by the Ó Máille in A.D. 1224. The church, which consists of a nave and chancel, was restored about 1480, when the ceiling was painted. There is a room over the chancel, and there was another building along the north wall of the nave. Except for a seventeenth-century monument in the chancel, inscribed with the arms of Ó Máille, there is little to notice in the church, the most important feature being the remains of paintings on the ceiling and west wall. So few painted walls have retained their designs in Irish churches that any traces that can be found are of interest. Another building on the island that deserves mention is the peel tower beside the harbour at the north-east corner of the island; it owes its interest to the fact that it is supposed to have been built by Grace O'Malley. The legends of this famous lady, who is credited with all kinds of wonderful exploits by sea and land, belong to the folk-lore of the island. Historically, she appears as Grainne ní Mháille. She was a daughter of Dubhdara Ó Máille, chieftain of Upper Owle Ó Máille (Murrisk). She first married Domhnall Ó Flaithbhertaigh, and secondly Richard an Iarainn Bourke, chief of Carra and Burrishoole. Her life was adventurous: she was captured by Gerald earl of Desmond, in 1577, and was imprisoned for a year and a half. On the whole she appears to have been friendly to the English in Ireland, and on one occasion is said to have had an interview with Queen Elizabeth. One of her sons, Theobald Bourke, was created earl of Mayo in 1628. Sir Henry Sidney described her as a most famous feminine sea captain called Granny Imally.

The island of Inisglora contains extensive remains of a monastery, comprising the cashel, three churches, three cells, and various crosses and gravestones. It lies off the coast of Erris, and forms part of the parish of Kilmore. The principal oratory, which is known as the chapel of St Breanainn, measures 12 ft. by 8 ft., it is built of dry-stone masonry with walls sloping inwards. The walls are about 3 ft. thick, with a west doorway having inclined jambs and a lintel. The other churches are respectively named *Teampull na Naomh* (the Saints Church), which is built of cemented masonry, and is later in date than St Breanainn's Chapel; and *Teampull na mban* (the church of the women). The cells are of the ordinary beehive type built of dry-stone masonry with the walls sloping inwards; one is known as St Breanainn's Cell. The cashel which encloses the monastery is 156 ft. in diameter, the walls have been much damaged, and little of them remain.

On Iniskea Islands (north and south) there are churches; that on the northern island being dedicated to St Columba. It is a small building of the usual early Irish type; an ancient bell was found amongst its ruins. There are on the north island a number of shell mounds in which bone needles and bronze pins have been found.

Achill Island, off the coast of Mayo, contains no ecclesiastical antiquities of interest, but a curious group of megalithic remains is to be seen on the island.

Caher Island, also off the Mayo coast, contains the remains of an early monastic settlement. The ruins consist of a small church dedicated to St Patrick, and some crosses. The oratory, which is in a fair state of preservation, measures 17 ft. by 14 ft. The east window appears to be of early date, but the doorway is considered to be later. St Patrick's bed is under the east gable of the church; it is a stone block carved with a large and smaller crosses.

Árdoileán (High Island) is situated off the coast of Connemara about 4 miles from *Inisbófinne*. It contains the ruins of a primitive monastery, the principal remain being the church, a small rectangular building of dry-stone masonry. The monastery was founded about A.D. 640 by St Féichin. Colgan obtained the oldest documents for his life of St Féichin from MSS. written at Árdoileán and Omey.

St Mac Dara's Island, in the parish of Moyrus, Co. Galway, lies west of Ard Bay. St Mac Dara is reputed to have lived in the sixth century ; the remains of his oratory, built of large stones, are to be seen. Some interesting sculptured crosses may also be observed on the island.

Aran Islands : the great forts for which the Aran Islands are celebrated have been described in the section dealing with the fortifications of this province ; their ecclesiastical antiquities also deserve some mention. On Inishmore, the North Island, are the ruins of *Teampull Breacain*, a church which formed part of a monastery. It is a large building, which has been altered in recent times, consisting of a nave and chancel divided by a semicircular chancel arch. The window in the north wall is primitive, that in the east end is slightly pointed ; while that in the south side of the chancel is attributed to the tenth century. There are several inscribed grave slabs to the north-east of the church. West of the church is Brecan's Bed (*Leaba Breacain*), at the west end of which is the shaft of a cross carved on one side with the Crucifixion, and on both sides with interlacings. The remains of the monastery are of little interest, and the same remark applies to a late building known as *Teampull an Phuill* (the church of the hollow).

At Kilmurvey is another interesting group of ruins, the principal of which is *Teampull Mhic Duach*, an early building of massive masonry. It is called after Colman Mac Duach, who founded Kilmacduagh in the seventh century. The remains consist of a chancel and nave.

Another group of ruins at Killeany includes two churches (all that now remain out of six), the base of a round tower, and the shaft of a High Cross. There are also the remains of the Franciscan Convent built in 1485. The remains of *Teampull Binein* and *Teglach*

Enda are interesting little churches of the type associated with early monastic settlements. *Teampull Enda* was founded by St Enda, who obtained a grant of Aran from Aonghus king of Cashel, at the end of the fifth century.

The principal antiquities of *Inishmaan*, or Middle Island, are, the great fort of *Dún Chonchobhair* already described, *Teampull Cenanagh*, a small oblong church of early type, a dolmen, and a stone fort called *Dún na mbothar*.

Inisheer, or South Island, contains an interesting oratory called Kilgobnet; the ruins of the church of St Cavan, *Teampull Choemhain*; and a large stone fort with a dry-stone turret known as O'Brien's Castle.

HIGH CROSSES

The High Crosses of this province, about twenty-one in number, are distributed as follows : Galway, nine ; Leitrim, one ; Mayo, four ; Roscommon, three ; and Sligo, four. The most remarkable of these being the crosses at Drumcliff (*Druim Cliabh*), Co. Sligo, and at Tuam, Co. Galway.

The High Cross at Drumcliff is situated beside the road to Bundoran, 4 miles north of Sligo, close to the Church and Round Tower. The cross, which is 13 ft. in height, is richly carved with figure scenes and ornamental patterns. The panels on the west face are curious ; the first is filled with interlaced work, the second represents three figures, the centre of whom is a bearded man holding an infant : the scene is conjectured to represent the presentation of Christ at the Temple. Above this is a grotesque animal in high relief ; then three figures, the scene being thought to represent the smiting of Christ ; above this are two figures which have not been interpreted. On the head of the Cross is the Crucifixion, with the lance and sponge. On the east face the lowest panel repre-

Drumcliff High Cross

sents Adam and Eve with the serpent, and the Tree of Knowledge whose roots and branches are wonderfully interlaced. Above this is an animal in high relief ; then Cain killing Abel ; next comes Daniel in the lions' den ; and on the head of the cross is the figure of a mitred archbishop, carrying a cross. There are cherubs' heads with interlacing on the arms and ring. The sides of the cross are ornamented with fret patterns, spiral patterns, and figures of animals, and, on the south arm-end of the cross, is the figure of the Virgin and Child.

The High Cross at Tuam is situated in the centre of the town. It is a ringed cross measuring some 14 ft. in height. The Crucifixion in high relief is carved on one side of the head, and the effigy of a bishop on the other. The shaft is decorated with interlaced patterns in low relief. The base has on one side two figures of ecclesiastics, and one in high relief on the other. There are four inscriptions on the cross, which may be dated to the first half of the twelfth century.

ARCHITECTURE

Monastic Foundations

Ware (1654) gives a list of nearly eighty monastic institutions of various kinds as having formerly existed in the province of Connaught. The remains of many of these present features of architectural and antiquarian interest, but it has been impossible to include descriptions of more than a few of the more important ruins.

Clare-Galway: the Franciscan convent of Clare-Galway, situated about 6 miles from Galway, was erected by John de Cogan in A.D. 1290. The convent was also richly endowed by the Bermingham family. The original church was built in the style of the thirteenth century. In plan it consists of a nave, with a north aisle, a square tower, north transept, and a chancel. The conventual buildings lie to the south. Owing to the convent having been inhabited after the dissolution down to as late as 1765, the buildings are in an unusually good state of preservation, but they have been much altered and added to. Close to the convent is Clare-Galway Castle : formerly a strong fortress, it was one of the many citadels of the De Burgos.

The Dominican Friary at Athenry was founded in

Dominican Friary, Athenry

A.D. 1241 by Meyler de Bermingham second baron of Athenry, who died in 1252, and was buried in the precincts of the friary. A house for scholars was founded in the friary by Finghin Mac Floind arch-bishop of Tuam in 1256. In 1423 the church was accidentally burnt, a bull for its repair being issued by Pope Martin V and renewed by Eugene IV in 1445. Queen Elizabeth granted the buildings to the portreeve and corporation of Athenry at a yearly rent. For a

brief period dating from 1644 the house was made a
university. In the eighteenth century it was utilised
as a barracks. Nothing remains of the friary except
the church, which stands in a neglected graveyard.
The church, in its present state, dates from 1324, when
it was reconstructed chiefly through the benefactions
of William de Burgos and his wife. It consists of a
nave with a north aisle and transept, and a chancel,
with a sacristy to the south. The east window is
interesting on account of the tracery; some of the
other windows also show tracery of good design. The
church contains a number of monuments, but no inscribed tomb of older date than the seventeenth century
is now to be seen.

The Connaught family of Bermingham was of importance. Thomas de Bermingham, baron of Athenry,
who died in 1376, caused the *Fiacail Phâdraig* or
Shrine of St Patrick's Tooth to be made. This shrine,
now preserved in the National Museum, Dublin, is made
of silver; it is richly decorated with figures in bas-relief,
settings of crystals, coloured glass, and amber. On its
front face is the Crucifixion in full relief, accompanied
by figures in low relief of the Saints, Benan, Patrick,
Columcille, and Brendan. The cruciform design on the
back contains among other figures a representation of
King David playing the harp. The shrine, which was
made to contain a tooth of St Patrick, is mentioned in
a seventeenth-century account of Connaught as the most
venerated relic in the province. A Latin inscription
on its front face records that Thomas de Bermingham,
lord of Athenry, caused it to be ornamented. Beneath
the lower portion of the silver plate in the front of the
shrine is inserted a piece of linen, doubtless a relic.

Church of Athenry Friary

H

The remains of the Dominican Friary at Roscommon
are interesting, chiefly on account of the altar tomb
of King Feidlimidh Ó Conchobhair (Phelim O'Conor),
which is situated under an arch on the north side of

Fiacail Phádraig (Shrine of St Patrick's Tooth)

the choir. The remains consist of a nave, chancel,
and transept. The church measures 138 ft. in length
and 25 ft. in width. It contains the remains of four
piers, with capitals, which formed an arcade separating
the nave from the north aisle. The window over the
main entrance is worthy of note. The tower and some

walls of the church were removed for building material in 1794. The chief monument, as above mentioned, is the tomb of Feidlimidh Ó Conchobhair, king of Connaught. King Feidlimidh founded the Convent in A.D. 1253, and was buried within its walls in 1265. His altar tomb has a slab at the top, carved with an effigy ; it is 7 ft. in length, and represents a figure of the king clothed in a long loose robe which reaches from the neck to the ankles, the sleeves are close-fitting. The head of the figure is crowned, and the right hand holds a sceptre headed with a *fleur-de-lis* ; the left arm clasps a crucifix ; the feet, clad in pointed shoes, rest on a hound. The effigy may be as old as the date claimed for it, *i.e.* the latter part of the thirteenth century, but the altar tomb on which it rests is not earlier than the fourteenth or fifteenth century. The front side of the tomb is divided into two halves : each half contains the figures of four *Gallóglaigh*, or heavy-armed foot soldiers, standing in a niche. The figures, with one exception, are all dressed and armed in a similar manner. They wear conical helmets, and shirts of chain mail reaching to the knees, beneath which appears a quilted garment and sleeves. Except for one, who holds a battle-axe, all carry broadswords. The tomb is interesting as showing the armour worn in Ireland at that period.

Boyle Abbey, Co. Roscommon, is a ruin of considerable interest. It was founded for Cistercians by Muirgheas Ó Dubhthaich in A.D. 1161, but it was built slowly, not being consecrated until 1220. Boyle Abbey is a good example of Irish Transitional architecture. The church was cruciform with an aisled nave, transepts with eastern chapels, and a chancel with a square tower at the junction of the nave and chancel. The cloisters and conventual buildings, of which the ruins are considerable, lie to the south. A portion of the southern arcade is Norman, probably it represents the remains of the unfinished Norman church which survived the fire of 1202. The similarity between the round pillars at Boyle, with their octagonal scalloped capitals carrying round arches, and English Norman work is so striking that it has been suggested that English workmen may have been responsible for them. The rest of the church is Transitional, the decoration of many of the capitals being elaborate and beautiful.

The Cistercian Abbey of Knockmoy, notable on account of the remains of wall-paintings still to be seen on its walls, is a picturesque ruin. Known as *Monasterium Collis Victoriæ*, it is situated on Knockmoy hill, about 6 miles to the south-east of Tuam, Co. Galway. It was founded in A.D. 1189 or 1190 by Cathal Ó Conchubhair king of Connaught, who himself entered the monastery, and, having died in the habit of a grey friar, was buried within its walls in 1224. The church is cruciform with an aisled nave, transepts which have the eastern square-headed chapels customary in Cistercian churches, and a chancel. A tower probably stood at the intersection of the nave and chancel, but no remains of it can now be traced. The chancel arch is pointed, those at the crossing are round. The vaulted chancel had a room over it. The interior of the church is plain, though it contains some ornate carving. It is an interesting example of Irish Transitional architecture, resembling in this respect the abbeys of Boyle and Corcomroe. The conventual buildings and cloister lay to the south. The fresco on the north wall of the chancel near the east window has often been described. It is divided into two scenes. The upper shows three crowned skeletons and three crowned kings carrying hawks. This scene represents the mediæval morality known as the three dead and three living kings. The lower compartment depicts the familiar story of St Sebastian's martyrdom. St Sebastian is shown bound to a tree with numerous arrows sticking through his body, on each side is an archer with a long bow in the act of letting fly an arrow. On the dexter side is a bearded, nimbed figure, having one hand raised in benediction, and the other holding what looks like the arm of a cross. The figure probably represents the Trinity, but the design is too much defaced to enable its details to be exactly distinguished.

Cong Abbey, situated at Ashford, Co. Galway, though not an extensive ruin, is worth attention on account of its architecture, which belongs to the Transitional period. A church is stated to have been founded at Cong by St Féichin in the seventh century, but the present foundation dates from the late twelfth century, when the abbey was built by Ruaidhri Ó Conchubhair, the last Irish king of Ireland. The church has a fine north doorway : its floor is covered with a number of gravestones of various dates. It was of the usual cruciform type with a square tower. The cloisters, which have been much restored, are an interesting example of Transitional work.

The Cross of Cong, now preserved in the National Museum, Dublin, was made about A.D. 1123 by Turlough Ó Conchubhair, king of Connaught, to enshrine a portion of the true Cross. It seems to have been originally made for the church of Tuam, being probably transferred from thence to the Augustinian abbey of Cong by either Archbishop Muiredach Ó Dubhthaich or King Ruaidhri Ó Conchubhair (Roderic O'Conor). It was thereafter preserved in Cong Abbey, becoming one of the chief relics of Ireland. It was presented in 1839 to the Royal Irish Academy by Professor MacCullagh ; he had purchased it from the last Abbot of Cong, who represented the Augustinian order in Connaught. The cross, now one of the most precious Christian antiquities preserved in the National Museum, Dublin, is a processional cross. It is made of oak encased with copper plates, decorated with ornaments of gilt bronze ; the sides, framed in silver, have incised upon them an inscription in Irish and Latin. The front of the cross is divided into a number of small panels, filled with zoomorphic ornament. In the centre is a large crystal : it was probably beneath this that was placed the relic. The back of the cross is covered by bronze plates decorated with zoomorphic ornament.

Kilconnell Monastery, Co. Galway, founded in A.D. 1414 for Franciscan monks by William O'Kelly, is one of the most perfect of the ancient houses of this Order now to be seen in Ireland. The remains consist of the church which has a nave with a south aisle, a south transept with an eastern chapel, and a choir. There is a square tower at the intersection of the nave and choir. This graceful tower is an especially beautiful feature of the church ; it is later than the original building, and has a groined roof. The cloister and conventual buildings lie to the north. The cloisters on the north side of the tower and eastern side of the garth are in good repair. An interesting tomb near the west door in the nave of the church is divided in front into six niches, each containing the effigy of a saint with their names inscribed above. The tomb is crowned by a beautiful flamboyant canopy, the finial of which is divided into two panels containing the figures of a bishop and another ecclesiastic. Several other tombs of interest are to be seen in the church, and the arms

Kilconnell Friary

of the following families are depicted on some of the later monuments: Bytagh, Barnewell, O'Daly, Ward, and O'Kelly. The convent was occupied and in good repair as late as the time of James I, its present exceptional state of preservation being due to this.

The Dominican Friary, generally called the Abbey of Sligo, was founded in A.D. 1252 by Maurice Fitz Gerald, who also built Sligo Castle. The town and friary were destroyed by fire on several occasions. In 1416 Pope John XXIII granted indulgences to all who should visit the friary and contribute to its repair : it was rebuilt in that year by Bryan Mac Donogh. After the dissolution the friary was granted to Sir William Taaffe. It has recently been vested in the Board of Works as a national monument. The church consists of a nave and choir, with a south transept and a tower at the division of the nave and choir : the conventual buildings lie to the north. There are some interesting tombs of seventeenth-century date in the church, the large monument in the choir to O'Conor Sligo being the most remarkable.

The Friary of Creevelea, near Dromahair, Co. Leitrim, was founded in 1508 by Margaret O'Rorke for Franciscan Friars Observant. The church consists of a nave and choir, with a tower at their intersection, and a south transept. The domestic buildings lie to the north. Some interesting carvings are to be seen on the pillars of the cloisters.

Cathedrals [1]

The province contains six cathedral churches, two of which, Clonfert, and Kilmacduagh, are ancient, while two others, Tuam, and Killala, are interesting.

Clonfert (*Cluain-fearta*, the meadow of the grave) is situated about 3 miles from Eyrecourt in Co. Galway. The bishopric was founded in A.D. 558 by St Breanainn. It was united with the See of Kilmacduagh in 1601, and by the Church Temporalities Act the Sees of Kil-

---

[1] The writer has received assistance in writing these notes on the cathedrals from *Cathedral Churches of Ireland*, 1894, by the late T. M. Fallow, F.S.A.

laloe and Kilfenora were also added to it. Clonfert is
less known than it deserves ; it possesses some interesting features, while its west door is one of the finest
specimens of Romanesque architecture in Ireland.
The cathedral is a small building, consisting of a nave
with a western tower, a chancel and a vaulted sacristy
to the north of this. Portions of the south transept
remain, but the north transept has disappeared. The
east gable of the chancel, considered to date from the
end of the tenth century, is probably the oldest portion
of the building. The western door is usually assigned
to the eleventh century. The east window has two
lights and is well proportioned. The chancel arch and
nave, which belong to the fifteenth century, have a
number of curious devices carved over them. The
celebrated western doorway, which has never been dis-
turbed and still shows its inclined jambs, is the finest
of its kind in Ireland. It consists of a round arch of
five orders, the columns being alternately round and
octagonal. The decoration of these is most ornate. The
innermost arch, next to the door, is considered to be of
later date than the others ; it shows ornamentation
characteristic of the Tudor period. Above the arch is a
triangular pediment ornamented with an arcade of six
columns, having round arches and a human head above
each : above this the space is filled with triangular
panels, alternately raised and sunk. The sunk panels
contain human heads, the top three and lower four being
bearded, while the remaining row of three are clean-
shaven. The raised panels are carved with leaf work.

Kilmacduagh, Co. Galway : the bishopric of Kilmacduagh was founded by St Colman in the seventh
century. St Colman, who was the son of Dui, was

known as Mac Duach to distinguish him from others of the name. The bishopric founded by him was named in consequence of this *Cill Mhic Duach* (the church of the son of Dui). The walls of Kilmacduagh Cathedral are still standing, but the building is roofless. It consists of a nave and chancel with transepts. It was rebuilt in the fifteenth century, to which period the principal part of the nave, chancel, and transepts belong. The round tower adjoining the cathedral inclines to one side, and in certain positions appears to be falling over ; its upper portion is a modern restoration, the lower is ancient.

Window in O'Heyne Monastery, Kilmacduagh

The cathedral of Tuam (*Tuaim*, a tumulus), the ecclesiastical capital of Connaught, is an interesting building. The see was founded in the sixth century by St Iarlaithe. The oldest remains of the present cathedral date from about A.D. 1152, when the cathedral was rebuilt by the assistance of Toirdelbhach Ó Conchubhair king of Ireland. The ancient portions are the chancel, with its three circular-headed windows, and the magnificent Romanesque arch. In 1860 the cathedral was rebuilt, by the late Sir Thomas Deane, in the style of Irish First-pointed architecture : he included in the rebuilding the ancient archway and windows. The chapter house contains some fine Renaissance stall-work, obtained on the Continent and presented to the diocese. The Romanesque arch is comprised externally of six semicircular, circular, and recessed arches. The shafts of the columns, except the outermost on each side, are semicircular and plain, but their rectangular capitals are richly

Round Tower at Kilmacduagh

carved with interlaced work, and in some cases with human heads.

Killala, Co. Mayo : the See of Killala (*Cell Aladh*) was founded by St Patrick, who consecrated an aged man of his household, Muiredach, as bishop. There are no traces of the earlier cathedral churches left, as the building that survived the Reformation was practically destroyed during the seventeenth century : the present cathedral was erected by Thomas Otway, consecrated bishop of Killala and Achonry in 1670. It is a plain rectangle in plan, with a square tower

Romanesque Arch, Tuam Cathedral

topped by a stone spire. A doorway in the south wall appears to be the only remnant of the ancient building. The See of Killala has been merged in that of Tuam since 1834.

The see of Elphin was also founded by St Patrick in his tour through Connaught : he appointed Assicus its first bishop. The present cathedral possesses no features of interest. The mediæval church was demolished in the seventeenth century: it was rebuilt in the later part of the same century by Bishop Parker. The actual building, with the exception of the tower, is probably of eighteenth-century date. It is a plain rectangle in plan, with a high square tower at the west, and an apse at the east end. The interior of the cathedral contains stalls for the chapter and the bishop's throne. Just on the outskirts of the town are the ruins of the bishop's palace.

Enachdune, now called Annaghdown, about 8 miles from Galway, on the shores of Lough Corrib, was formerly the seat of a bishopric. A small and unimportant see from its foundation, its bishops often acted as assistant bishops in English dioceses. The matrix of the seal of Gilbert bishop of Enachdune, 1306–24, who was suffragan to the Bishop of Coventry, is in the collection of the Royal Irish Academy. The see became absorbed in that of Tuam at an early date. Some ecclesiastical ruins are still to be seen at Annaghdown.

Castles

The town of Galway, which as a commercial city once ranked second to Dublin, is now decayed; it is interesting on account of its numerous ancient houses and castellated mansions. Of these Lynch's Castle, built in the Tudor style, may be noticed: it is in good preservation; the ornamental details above the windows, and some heraldic medallions let into the walls, are worth attention. The collegiate church of St Nicholas, Galway, founded in 1320, is one of the finest churches in Ireland: it consists of a choir, nave with side aisles, and a square tower on which a steeple was erected in 1683. The church contains many monuments of interest.

Castles are numerous in Connaught. Some 270 are enumerated for Galway alone in a list compiled in 1574, contained in one of the Carew MSS. Many of these belonged to the Bourkes. The Galway castles are small : they generally consist of a rectangular keep, forming the defensive portion of the building, with an attached enclosure, called a bawn, guarded by a wall.

Lynch's Castle, Galway

The castle at Athenry, called King John's or Bermingham Castle, is of this type, but stronger. Much of the ancient town wall of Athenry still remains.

Fiddaun Castle, about 2 miles from Tubber railway station, on the line between Athenry and Limerick, is remarkable for the large bawn enclosing it, the space enclosed being some 128 ft. by 80 ft. : the walls, which are about 5 ft. thick and 12 ft. high, are loopholed for

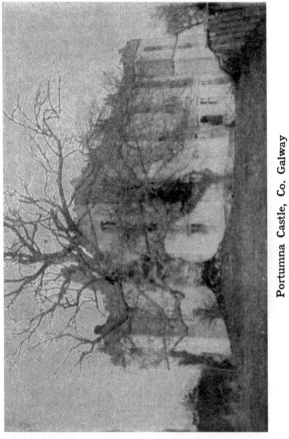

Portumna Castle, Co. Galway

musketry. The castle was one of three belonging to the O'Shaughnessys.

Pallas Castle, near Loughrea, is well preserved: it also has a bawn which is in good repair.

Roscommon Castle, built by Robert de Ufford in 1269, is a quadrangular building with a tower at each corner and two more at the gateway: it measures 220 ft. by 173 ft., in extent. The towers, which are

Roscommon Castle

circular externally, measure 20 ft. in radius: the vaulted roofs are of great strength.

Ballintubber Castle, Roscommon, an extensive ruin, was also quadrangular in plan, with four angle towers.

Ballymote Castle, Co. Sligo, built in 1300 by Richard de Burgos earl of Ulster, was a large and strong building flanked by six round towers enclosing an extensive courtyard: its entrance was defended by earthworks.

ADMINISTRATION

THE province of Connaught includes the counties of Galway, Leitrim, Mayo, Sligo, and Roscommon, of which the first four are maritime, Roscommon being the only inland county. The province, speaking generally, is poor, and in many districts the land is hardly capable, under present conditions, of supporting the population; and when there is a failure of crops, especially the potato crop, great hardship is experienced. The population has very greatly decreased during recent years. According to the census of 1841 there were in Connaught no fewer than 1,418,859 persons. In subsequent censuses this number has undergone steady diminution, until in 1911 the population had been reduced to 610,984. The decline in population is to be attributed largely to emigration, for up to 1918 no fewer than 731,218 persons had emigrated from the province, and of this number females slightly preponderated over males. The greater number of the emigrants went to the United States of America. It should also be remarked that Connaught has contributed the great bulk of those migratory agricultural labourers who annually leave their homes to work at a distance, many going to England and Scotland for harvesting operations. Thus in the year 1914 no fewer than 5438 migratory labourers left the province, and went to England and Scotland. The great majority of these came from Co. Mayo.

The total rateable value of the province is nearly £1,500,000, out of a total of nearly £16,000,000 for the whole of Ireland.

I

Irish is still spoken in many parts of the province, and according to the census of 1911, there were over 217,000, or over 35 per cent. of the population, who could speak Irish, while over 9000 persons could speak Irish only.

The population of the province, and other data are shown in the accompanying table.

(1)	Population. (Census of 1911.) (2)	Area on which the Valuation has been determined. (3)	Valuation on 1st March 1914. (4)
		Acres.	£
Maritime Counties			
Galway—			
Rural Districts	163,800	1,510,862	446,879
Urban Districts	18,424	9,590	40,020
Leitrim—			
Rural Districts	63,582	392,369	139,212
Mayo—			
Rural Districts	190,143	1,377,286	308,504
Urban Districts	2,034	4,067	21,406
Sligo—			
Rural Districts	67,882	449,330	192,866
Urban Districts	11,163	3,008	23,364
Inland County			
Roscommon—			
Rural Districts	93,956	631,684	303,431

Prior to 1922 the province returned fourteen Parliamentary representatives. By the Redistribution of Seats Act of 1918, the borough of Galway was merged in the county, which then returned four members.

There was appointed for each county one of H.M.
Lieutenants, together with a number of Deputy
Lieutenants.

Since 1883 legislation has permitted operations
having for their object the improvement of housing
conditions. A great forward step was taken by an
Act of 1890, and since then other Acts have been passed,
making the total sum available for the purpose some
£6,250,000. In all, about 48,000 labourers' cottages have
been built in Ireland. This work has been done by
the Rural District Councils under the guidance of the
Local Government Board. A large part of this valuable
work has been carried out in Connaught, where the
housing conditions have been enormously improved.
Many of the mud-walled, ill-thatched cabins which
dotted Connemara, and indeed the whole province,
in which the single room was often enough shared with
a cow or a pig, have been replaced by well-built cottages,
each with its own piece of land attached. The important
work of the Congested Districts Board in this connexion
is dealt with later.

EDUCATION

The sparsely populated condition of the counties
which constitute the province of Connaught, with its
large tracts of lake, mountain, and bog, and the agricultural pursuits of the bulk of the inhabitants, have
dictated the nature and limitations of the educational
facilities in the area. Scattered over it there are some
1422 National Schools, in which, in addition to the " three
Rs," other elementary subjects are taught, including,
in some schools, rural science and school gardening,

and, in girls' schools, domestic economy.   In nearly 400 schools Irish is taught, and instruction through the medium of Irish is given in about ninety " bilingual " schools.   In this connection it may be noted that in a large number of centres in the province, classes in Irish for teachers in National Schools have been formed under schemes administered by the Department of Agriculture and Technical Instruction.

The province is well supplied with secondary schools, and, though there are Protestant secondary schools in Galway and Sligo, the much larger Roman Catholic population has called for the establishment of schools suited to its needs, for while the National Schools of Ireland are, in principle, undenominational in character, the secondary schools are frankly denominational.   In the town of Galway are three Catholic secondary schools for boys, St Ignatius' College, St Joseph's Seminary, and St Mary's College ; while the Dominican Convent at Taylor's Hill is a distinguished school for Catholic girls.   St Joseph's College at Ballinasloe is an important boys' school.   In Co. Roscommon there is, at Ballagha- derreen, a college for Catholic boys, and in the town of Sligo there is the important Summerhill College, and, for girls, the Ursuline Convent School.   The last men- tioned school provides a generous education, in which for many years past there has been successful teach- ing of experimental science and domestic economy. There is attached to this school a Higher School of Domestic Economy, to which girls who have received a general secondary education are admitted for a further year's training in domestic economy.   Mention may also be made of the Municipal Day Trades Preparatory School, which is conducted at the Technical School,

Ursuline Convent, Sligo

under the management of the Technical Instruction Committee of the Urban Council.

Nor is the province without its facilities for education of University type, for we have in the city of Galway a University College, which is a constituent college of the National University of Ireland. It may be recalled that by an Act of 1845 this College was one of the three Queen's Colleges established, the other two being in Belfast and Cork. These colleges were similar in constitution and were undenominational. Their students were eligible for degrees granted by the Queen's University, which was incorporated about the same time. The Queen's University and Colleges ran a short and troubled course ; they were denounced as " godless institutions," and in 1854 the Irish Roman Catholic Hierarchy established a Catholic University of Ireland in order to provide education of university character of which they could approve. After considerable controversy, the Queen's University was dissolved under the University (Ireland) Act of 1879. The Queen's Colleges were not affected by this, and by royal charter granted in 1880 the Royal University of Ireland was established, the function of which was to act as an examining body for the Queen's Colleges. On the passing of the Irish University Act of 1908 the Royal University was dissolved and the National University established, and the Queen's College of Galway became a constituent college of the new university. The site of the University College occupies about fourteen acres. There are seven faculties, viz., Arts, Celtic, Science, Law, Medicine, Engineering, and Commerce. There is a two years' course in agricultural science, co-ordinated with the Faculty of Agriculture in the Royal College

University College, Galway

of Science, Dublin. Valuable scholarships and exhibitions are offered by the governing body, while a number of County and County-Borough Councils grant scholarships tenable at this institution. Such of these scholars as take agriculture are admitted for one year as agricultural apprentices to the Department's Agricultural Station at Athenry, in order to prepare for the prescribed examinations in practical agriculture.

The great majority of youths leave the elementary school at a comparatively early age, and for them, in recent years, increasing efforts have been made by the Department of Agriculture and Technical Instruction to provide such supplementary instruction as is possible, for the most part in evening classes. Permanent centres of instruction are only possible in the larger centres, and technical schools have been established in Galway, Sligo, Ballinasloe and Ballina. The fundamental subjects of the courses of instruction in these centres are English, elementary mathematics, manual instruction, drawing, and elementary science ; these subjects being taken in an introductory course provided for those who have received an elementary education only. In each of these schools courses of commercial instruction and domestic training are also given, while Sligo and Galway make provision for instruction in science, technology, and art. Organised courses such as those referred to are only possible in the larger centres, and the number of them is increasing ; but there are many would-be students living at such distances from these centres that it is not possible for them to take advantage of the facilities offered by them. Every county in the province, however, has a Technical Instruction Committee, which provides under its scheme itinerant courses of instruction which are carried out in small and remote villages. Many of these courses deal with manual instruction in wood. The instruction consists of applied drawing, the use of wood-working tools, the nature of different timbers, and the application of this knowledge to the making of useful articles. This instruction is supplemented in some centres by courses in building construction, and the teachers of these classes have, for the most part, been especially trained by the Department. Their training is continued and supplemented by summer courses of instruction held at the Royal College of Science and the Metropolitan School of Art, Dublin, every year in the month of July. The local courses are held in any suitable building, the equipment being temporarily installed therein. The courses last for at least six weeks, and in many cases for a longer period, according to the nature of the demand. In a similar manner local courses of instruction are arranged in cookery and other forms of household work. In a number of centres courses are held in elementary commercial subjects, for which there is an increasing demand. Courses in hygiene and first aid are given in Cos. Roscommon and Galway, and in this manner instruction of a practical character, suited to their needs, has been made available to dwellers in remote rural districts.

In this educational work in rural districts every effort is made to adapt the character of the instruction to the needs of each district. In Co. Galway, for example, an Irish-speaking domestic economy instructress has made a special study of local needs in the remoter districts, which it is difficult to deal with under the more normal schemes. She resides in a cottage in the district, and not only visits the homes of the people, but brings them to her own cottage to demonstrate the practical application of her lessons. The dietary of the people in these remote parts is often unnecessarily monotonous, the principal meal of the day usually consisting of potatoes and cabbage, with the occasional addition of bacon. Turnips, peas, or carrots are seldom used, and fruit almost never. The object of the teaching is, in part, to improve the dietary and to introduce the use of a greater variety of vegetables, and considerable improvements have resulted. Seeds have been supplied, the cultivation of the vegetables explained and the various methods of cooking them carried out by such simple means as exist in the homes of the people. A teacher similarly qualified as regards language has given valuable and much-needed instruction in first aid and hygiene on the Aran Islands.

Nuns of the Presentation Convent at Keel, in Achill Island, have been specially trained in domestic economy, and are now giving more thorough and personal instruction in homecraft than is possible in the occasional visits of itinerant teachers.

The County Schemes of Technical Instruction usually include scholarships, which enable selected girls to proceed to convent residential schools of domestic economy for a period of one year.

In addition to this there are in operation central and county scholarship schemes, which enable boys of promise to continue their education in Trades Preparatory Schools in the larger centres of population, and in special courses for apprentices organised by the Department.

In various centres instruction has been given in different forms of home industry. Certain convent schools have at times established classes in lace and crochet making, needlework, knitting, and other subjects. The convent in Tuam was a pioneer in work of this nature.

In the matter of agricultural instruction reference has already been made to the Department's Agricultural Station at Athenry. This station provides training for young men who intend to follow farming. Those deemed suitable are taken on as apprentices. They are mainly engaged on outdoor work, being required to take part in all the work of the fields and farmyard. This is supplemented by class-room instruction, which is given, as a rule, in the evenings. The general education of the apprentices is not lost sight of. The training is particularly suitable for boys who have attended winter agricultural classes, organised by County Committees of Agriculture. Certain Committees award scholarships as a result of attendance at these classes, enabling the holders to continue their training at the Athenry station and other centres maintained by the Department. For this purpose the Department have approved of the college managed by the Franciscan Brothers at Mount Bellew, Co Galway, where a similar course of training is provided as for the Department's apprentices.

The County Committees of Agriculture referred to are, like the Technical Instruction Committees, statutory committees of the County Councils. In addition to providing instruction in agriculture, they carry out a large amount of teaching through the medium of their itinerant instructresses in dairying and poultry-keeping.

INDUSTRIES & MANUFACTURES

A GLANCE at the map of Connaught will serve to show
that one need not look for factory industries in the
province. Large areas of waste and bog-land, of lough
and mountain, scant railway and indifferent road
communications do not favour industrial enterprise.
With a few exceptions then, the industries are such as
one would expect, those which supply the needs of a
scanty population, or those formed to provide occasional or seasonal employment to supplement the slender
means of the peasantry. The portal towns of Sligo and
Galway, it is true, boast some important industries. In
Sligo the Connaught Manufacturing Company have for
some time carried on shirt-making on a fairly large scale,
and there is some coach-building and corn-milling. An
attempt was made nearly twenty years ago to establish
a wood-working industry, but with little success. A
very successful—one might almost say famous—venture
is the Lissadel Bulb Farm, a few miles from Sligo.
There is a considerable export of eggs from Sligo,
while considerable quantities of wheaten flour and
other foodstuffs are imported. The city of Galway
possesses a few industries. Once it was a place of
considerable importance and did a big trade with
Spain, but the population has greatly declined, and
factories now stand empty and in ruins. There are
still some factories which derive ample power from
the River Corrib. This water-power might be very
much developed for industrial purposes, and the
efficiency of its utilisation greatly increased. Galway
indeed possesses great potentialities. Its bay has been

declared by experts to be "the most suitable site for a great national harbour." Schemes have been urged for making Galway a great transatlantic port for a "through Ireland" route for mails and passengers to Canada, with a train ferry across the Irish Channel. It is pointed out that Galway is, through Holyhead, only about 15 hours from London, while the sea route to St John's, Newfoundland, is but 1656 miles, and to Halifax, 2165 miles.

Notwithstanding the decline referred to, there have been encouraging signs of an industrial revival. A large and flourishing woollen factory (manufacturing blankets, friezes, and "homespuns") has grown up during the last twenty years, starting in a small way, largely through the enthusiasm and active co-operation of the parish priest, with local capital. There is also some boat-building, while the Congested Districts Board are encouraging glove- and toy-making, and motor-engine repairing.

In Connemara, not far from the city of Galway, are the famous granite and marble quarries. Here is quarried the beautiful green "Serpentine," which has been widely used as an ornamental marble. Black marble is also quarried near Oughterard, and much of this has been exported to the Continent in past years.

Beyond these quarries the "mineral resources" of the province are not very considerable, but the existence of a coalfield in the area must be noticed. On the southern bank of Lough Allen, near the junction of the counties of Sligo, Leitrim, and Roscommon, is the coal area known as the Arigna Coalfield. The seams of semi-bituminous coal vary in thickness from 6 ins. to 2 ft. 6 ins., and the total actual reserves (including

the north and south Arigna and the Slieveanierin area)
amount to some 8,696,000 tons. A short narrow-gauge
line .3½ miles long has been laid, connecting the mine
with the Cavan and Leitrim Railway, which will permit
of a greatly increased output. Iron and lead ores
exist in the area, as also in Mayo, where there are also
valuable slate quarries.

More characteristic of the area are the cottage
and rural industries already referred to, which have
served so useful a part in ameliorating the lot of a
people whose trouble " is not the scarcity of land,
but the scarcity of any but the poorest land." The
conditions of life in many districts of the province,
especially in Connemara, were such as to call for a large
measure of Governmental assistance, and this was given.
Along the coast are the fisher folk who, in small boats
and even their frail coracles, engage in fishing, but
who supplement this by harvesting seaweed, which
is used for manurial purposes. Certain kinds of weed
contain a large percentage of iodine and potash.
These are collected and partially burnt, the resulting
product, known as "kelp," being sold to chemical
manufacturers, who extract the valuable substances
referred to. In 1915 Co. Galway produced some 2000
tons of kelp, smaller quantities coming from Mayo
and Sligo. This industry became more important during
the war, but in 1920 production fell to 780 tons. Efforts
are being made to organise the industry and to place
the marketing of the kelp on a better footing. Inland,
the greater number of the people engage in rural work ;
it can scarcely be called agricultural in many cases
—much of the land is not cultivable. Sheep- and cattle-
rearing is the predominant feature, and it is noteworthy

that there are as many sheep in the county of Galway as in the whole of the province of Ulster. These conditions led to the periodical excursions of "migratory labourers," who went in such large numbers at certain periods of the year from the West of Ireland to assist

Roscommon Hogget Rams

in harvesting operations in England and Scotland. The means of livelihood under such conditions are necessarily precarious. Failure of the potato crop involves great hardship, sometimes famine. The introduction of spraying, and the facilities given for its regular practice has, happily, greatly minimised this danger. Home industries which yield a contribution to the family budget are clearly much to be desired, and widespread efforts have been made to establish such industries, both by voluntary and Governmental agencies. The conditions referred to led the Government of the day to create, in 1891, the Congested Districts Board to deal specially with certain districts to be defined. The term " congested " is something of a misnomer as applied to a sparsely-populated area, but implies an area where the means of livelihood are insufficient to

Woollen Mills on the Shannon, Athlone

support its population. It was decided that the electoral division should be the unit of congestion, and that no division should be placed under the Board if the average rateable valuation per head exceeded 30s. Although at first the areas dealt with by the Board comprised only detached electoral divisions, the present " congested " districts include the whole of the province. The operations of the Board were confined to certain counties, and wide powers were conferred upon it, not only in regard to land-purchase and re-sale, to the encouragement of agriculture and fisheries, but also in regard to rural industries. One of the first acts of the Board in this connection was to assist the Foxford (Co. Mayo) Providence Woollen Mills, which

Hand-spinning, Achill Island

had been started by the Sisters of Charity, by a loan of £7000, and subsidies of over £8000 for the training of workers. They also gave capitation grants, amounting to over £4000, and a loan of £3000 to the Ballaghaderreen Hosiery Factory, which had also been started by the same Order. The Board also made

K

efforts to improve existing rural industries, like hand-spinning, weaving and knitting. Experts were employed, loans were made for the purchase of improved looms and spinning wheels, and instruction was given in weaving and dyeing. Great assistance was given to develop the lace and crochet industries. A large number of classes were started and assisted, and a very valuable supplement was thus made to the family income. When, in 1899, the Department of Agriculture and Technical Instruction was established, they developed, under similar powers, other centres, and gave aid to a large number of rural industries. Industries were started in the convent at Tuam, and lace, crochet, embroidery, machine knitting, etc., were developed and encouraged by grants for the purpose of training workers. Much good work has been done, and Irish lace and crochet, hand-embroidery, and other forms of handicraft have become famous. Among other centres of the lace and crochet industry in the province may be mentioned Benada, Tobercurry, and Cliffoney in Co. Sligo; Castlebar and Kiltimagh in Co. Mayo; and Oughterard and Derrypark in Co. Galway. The manufacture of home-spun and hand-woven woollens has been carried on in many centres, as at Westport (Co. Mayo) and Leenane (Co. Galway). The use of vegetable dyes for home-dyeing, which was common, has now become very rare, and the aniline (coal-tar) dyes are more commonly used.

AGRICULTURE

Taken as a whole, the province of Connaught is not an ideal agricultural district. Its area is 4,228,211 acres, of which 11.6 per cent. is under turf, bog, and marsh, while large areas consist of barren mountain-land. It is not surprising, therefore, to find that in 1916 it had a smaller proportion of land under cultivation than in any other province. Only some 7.1 per cent. was under corn and green crops, while 44.3 per cent. was under grass. Sheep are raised in large numbers, especially in Galway, and there were considerably over a million sheep in the province in 1916. There are relatively few cattle and remarkably few horses, the useful ass being found more suited to the conditions of the country. The far-reaching changes which the country experienced after the famine profoundly affected this western land. In 1851 some 360,000 acres were under corn crops. By 1916 these had decreased by 61.8 per cent.—that is, to a little over 137,000 acres. During the same period the acreage under hay had increased from 132,000 to 400,000 acres. The imperative demand for increased food supplies during the war led to a remarkable effort on the part of farmers throughout Ireland, and in this effort Connaught was by no means last. Between 1916 and 1918 Connaught increased its acreage of crops other than hay by nearly 147,000 acres, or 48.7 per cent. Potatoes are of course an important crop in the district, and the acreage of this crop was increased from 118,830 acres in 1916 to 155,863 acres in 1918.

The poverty of the land, aggravated by a vicious system of land tenure, brought the people living in these western districts into a condition of serious penury. In the areas scheduled as congested nine-tenths of the population live upon agricultural holdings. There were in 1908 84,954 holdings with a valuation of £523,188, which gives an average valuation of a little over £6 per holding ! Such holdings could scarcely be expected to support a family in any degree of comfort. On many estates in the West, where the cabins are clustered together in unbeautiful hamlets, and where the people have been in occupation for generations, the land is held in "rundale." In other parts the people have sub-divided their holdings to such an extent that an

Old type of cottage in the West of Ireland

efficient system of cultivation was rendered impossible. Small farms would consist of separate portions of land in many and far-removed positions. A field of one acre might belong to a dozen different persons. It was here that the Congested Districts Board initiated a great reform. When they bought such estates they "pooled" the land and redistributed it. The process of dividing the land into separate and distinct holdings

was known as "striping," and though there was
difficulty in commending the new arrangements to
those concerned, it was sometimes possible to give
a greater area of land to the tenant than before,
and to offer a well-built and sanitary cottage. An
enormous amount of assistance has been given, but

Type of Labourers' cottages with which the Congested
Districts Board are replacing the old insanitary cabins

the tenant was required to join with the Board in the
erection of houses on his own farm, supplying labour
and carts and, where possible, local material obtained
by his own labour. Many districts have been trans-
formed by such means. The process of resettlement
involved much constructive effort, such as the provision
of turbary, arterial drainage, roads, drains, fences, etc.

The resettlement of Clare Island is a case in point. This was bought in 1895 for £5000, and after resettling it, the Board resold to the tenants direct. At the time of purchase the greater part of the island was held in rundale, and few tenants knew where their land or their rights began or ended. There were no fences, cattle and sheep roamed the whole island, and land under crops had to be guarded against the incursions of cattle by members of the tenants' families. The first work undertaken was the building at a cost of £1600 of a stone wall, about five miles long, across the island, and separating cultivable land from the mountain grazing. Over fifty miles of fences were constructed from the wall to the sea, partitioning the cultivable land among the tenants. Other estates were dealt with in a similar manner. Agricultural development followed resettlement, and this was carried out by the Agricultural Branch of the Land Commission from 1891 until 1899, when much of it was transferred to the Department of Agriculture and Technical Instruction. The whole was transferred in 1904. This development work takes a number of different forms—mainly educational in character. Object lessons were furnished by the establishment of experimental plots and example holdings. Under the Department's schemes of agriculture for each county, instructors are appointed, and these carry out courses of instruction over the whole area. Under, for example, the Co. Galway Agricultural Scheme for 1920–21 we find such items as the following :

Fruit Trees and Shelter Belt Scheme.

Provision for Bee-keeping appliances for Connemara.

Encouragement of Poultry industry in Connemara.

Encouragement of Milk production.

Land resettled by the Congested Districts Board near Castlerea, Co. Roscommon

Cottage and Farm Prizes.

Live Stock Schemes (nomination of mares, premiums for bulls and boars).

In addition to subsidies to shows and ploughing matches, there is provision made for instruction in agriculture, horticulture, bee-keeping, poultry-keeping, and butter-making.

Working under the Department's programmes are the Schools of Rural Domestic Economy, the object of which is to train girls of the farming class in the work of their own homes. Such schools are to be found at Benada Abbey (Co. Sligo) ; Loughglynn, near Castlerea (Co. Roscommon) ; Claremorris, Swinford, and West-port (Co. Mayo) ; and at Clifden and Portumna (Co. Galway). The curriculum of these schools includes such subjects as dairying, poultry-keeping, cookery, and needlework.

Large parts of the province are unfavourable to the growth of timber, and in the whole area there are only about 48,000 acres under forest trees, of which nearly 23,000 acres are in Co. Galway. 106 acres were planted during the year ended 31st May 1916, the total number of trees planted being 245,205. By far the greater number of trees planted were conifers. Over 112,000 larch were planted, and over 86,000 fir, spruce, and pine. The greater number of plantations were in Galway, where over 128,000 trees were planted, over 15,000 ash, in addition to conifers, being put in.

An experiment in afforestation was made in 1890 by the Irish Government at Knockboy, near Carna, on the Connemara Coast. 820 acres of rough mountain and bog were purchased, mainly for the purpose 'of

School of Rural Domestic Economy, Westport

School of Rural Domestic Economy, Benada Abbey,
Co. Sligo

this experiment, but incidentally with the object of relieving local distress, for a deep bog had to be drained. A sum of £9000 was spent, but the experiment appears to have been a complete failure. Knockboy is but a couple of miles from the sea, and is a hillside facing S.W. open to the full strength of the Atlantic storms.

In 1907 a Departmental Committee on Irish Forestry was appointed, and this reported in April of the following year. Re-afforestation is now proceeding under expert direction. The Department of Agriculture and Technical Instruction have a Forestry Inspector and, in connection with the Royal College of Science, a Professor of Forestry.

FISHERIES

The sea and river fisheries of the province mean much to the population. The sea fisheries were of great importance long ago, but in the sixteenth century were mainly carried on by Spanish boats, and in the seventeenth century by the French and Dutch. It was not till the eighteenth century that the Irish Western fisheries became important to Ireland. It has been pointed out that, after the settlements of the seventeenth century, when the majority of the native race were compelled to depend for their food less on the produce of the flocks and herds, and more on potatoes, fish were sought after as a useful supplement to a potato diet, and the sea fisheries were worked with vigour. Later on bounties were introduced to stimulate the industry. The early years of the nineteenth century showed a decline in the catch of fish, and this decline was accentuated when the bounties were withdrawn in 1830. Soon after the famine there was a general collapse, there being no authority charged with the development of the fisheries. Commissioners had been established in 1819, but were abolished in 1830, and twelve years later the Board of Works became virtually the fishery authority. Some years later the industry was revolutionised by the introduction of steam vessels, and more rapid transit on the land. This and the use of ice for packing led to the delivery of fresh fish all over England, in places where it had been unknown before. This led to a great revival of the Irish sea fisheries. At a later period Inspectors of Irish fisheries were appointed, though at the time there were no funds to carry out fishery development. Later, funds were used for making loans of fishing boats. At the present time the administration of the fisheries is carried out by a branch of the Department of Agriculture and Technical Instruction, who apply funds for the protection and development of the industry. The assistance rendered by the Congested Districts Board and by the Department consists of the construction of marine works (piers, boatslips, lights, etc.), the advancing of loans for the purchase of boats, nets, and fishing gear, the promotion of boat-building and barrel-making, and the development of marketing facilities. In the earlier days the Board even acted as buyers and curers at different places until private enterprise came into play. They bought mackerel, herring, cod, and ling along the Mayo and Galway coast, and cured the fish or despatched it fresh. This work is now carried on by private firms. Encouragement was and is still rendered by instruction in fishery and in the care of nets, and, since the introduction of motor-boats, instruction has been given to

men in the management and running of motors. Instruction of this kind and in boat-building is at present
being developed in Galway.

Near this little city is the Claddagh, a picturesque
quarter of the fisher folk where many old customs
still persist.

But we look in vain along the Connaught coast

"Black Hookers," Sligo

for any concentrated fishing communities. We have
on the other hand numerous crofter fishermen, who
usually divide their energies between fishing and
the cultivation of their small holdings. Their fishing
equipment is usually small, and often takes the form
of canvas canoes, which, while they serve for catching
fish when they come, or for gathering seaweed, do

not allow them to go far from home. These canvas canoes can be carried by the crew into a place of safety, an important consideration on a coast fully exposed to the fury of Atlantic storms, where, it is said, waves have smashed lighthouse walls 200 ft. above sea level. The Galway fishing centres of Roundstone, Cleggan, and the Aran Islands engage with varying fortune in the spring and autumn mackerel fisheries.

There are eel fisheries in the Galway and Ballina districts, though not of great size. These two centres, together with Sligo, are important West Coast centres for salmon fishing.

DISTINGUISHED CONNAUGHT MEN

IF the number of distinguished men produced by Connaught falls below that of the other provinces, historical and geographical considerations amply account for it. There are few seats of learning, consequently a restricted professional class, and no industrial towns. Still, its record is considerable. It can claim some of the greatest of Irish antiquaries and, in Sir Gabriel Stokes, one of the most celebrated mathematicians of modern times.

COLMAN, Saint (d. 676), of Lindisfarne, was in all probability a native of Mayo. He studied at Iona, and was a member of the monastery there during the abbacy of Segene. In 661 he succeeded Finan as Bishop of Lindisfarne. He followed the early or Celtic mode of observing Easter, and adopted the Irish tonsure. At the synod of Whitby in 664, Oswin, king of Northumberland, who had hitherto sided with Colman, was persuaded by the arguments of the learned Wilfrid to give his adhesion to the Roman usage. Colman thereupon withdrew from Lindisfarne, with all his Irish, and a number of his English, monks. After a stay at Iona, some say four years, he returned to Ireland and founded a monastery on the little island of Innishbofin, off the coast of Mayo, and another in Magh Eo (Mayo) for his English monks. He died on Innishbofin.

CONRY, Florence (1560–1629), Archbishop of Tuam, in Irish Flaithrí Ó Maoilchonaire, was born in Galway, and studied in the Netherlands and at Salamanca, where he entered the Franciscan Order. A devoted student of St Augustine he published in Latin a *Commentary* on his works, and a *Compendium* of his teaching. Having obtained the favour of Philip II., he was appointed Provincial of the Irish Franciscans, and embarked on the ill-fated Armada, to which his *Peregrinus Jerichuntinus* (1641) alludes. He was largely instrumental in persuading Philip III. in 1616 to found the College of St Anthony at Louvain, afterwards famous as a seat of learning. When Hugh Roe O'Donnell lay dying at Simancas, Conry acted as his confessor. He never took over the see of Tuam to which he was appointed in 1609. He died in Madrid, his remains being translated to Louvain in 1654. The work by which he is best known is his *Emanuel* (1616), a treatise on Christian doctrine adapted from the Spanish, and justly regarded as a masterpiece of Irish prose.

CROKER, John Wilson (1780–1857), statesman and author, was born in Galway, and educated at Trinity College. He first came into notice by his *A Sketch of the*

State of Ireland Past and Present (1808), which ran through twenty editions, and immediately procured him the Chief Secretaryship of Ireland, in succession to Sir Arthur Wellesley, then appointed to the command in

John Wilson Croker

Spain. The following year he became Secretary to the Admiralty, and for twenty-two years directed its affairs with supreme ability. In Parliament he was a skilled debater, on more than one occasion eclipsing Macaulay, who retaliated by a severe criticism of Croker's edition of Boswell's *Life of Johnson* (1831). He was the trusted friend of Wellington, Peel, and

Canning, who several times urged him to accept high office in the cabinet. He finally broke with Peel over the abolition of the Corn Laws. As a literary man he is best known by his connection with *The Quarterly Review*, and the Athenaeum Club, both of which he was instrumental in founding.

KIRWAN, Richard, F.R.S. (1733–1812), chemist and mineralogist, was born at Cloughballymore, Co. Galway, and educated at Trinity College and at St Omer's. The "Nestor of English chemistry," his earliest experiments, which were on specific gravity and chemical affinity procured him the Copley Medal in 1782. His best work lay in the improvement of chemical analysis, inculcated in his remarkable *Essay on the Analysis of Mineral Waters* (1799). His *Elements of Mineralogy* (1784) was the first systematic treatment of the subject in English, and was for long the standard work, being translated into French, German, and Russian. He was President of the Royal Irish Academy from 1799 till his death in 1812.

LYNCH, John (1599–1673), Archdeacon of Tuam, was born in Galway, where his father kept a grammar school. He was ordained priest in France in 1622. When the Parliamentary forces entered Galway in 1652, he withdrew to France. There, at Saint Malo, he published in Latin, over the signature Gratianus Lucius, his best-known work *Cambrensis Eversus* (1662), dedicated to Charles II. Though nominally a refutation of Giraldus, its scope is much wider, and it remains a work of great value. He also executed a Latin translation of Keating's *History of Ireland*, still extant in MS. He died in France, probably at Saint Malo.

MAC FIRBIS, Duald (1585–1670), in Irish Dubhaltach Mac Firbisigh, Irish scholar and historian, was born in the Castle of Lackan, Co. Sligo, where his family were for generations hereditary historians and poets to the chief septs of Connaught, in particular to the Ó Dubhda, chiefs of Húi Fiachrach. His direct ancestor, Gilla Iósa Mór Mac Firbisigh, was the writer and compiler of the great *Book of Lecan* (1416), now in the Royal Irish Academy, and also of the *Yellow Book of Lecan* proper, in Trinity College. Duald's fame rests on his *Book of Genealogies* ("Craobha Coibhneasa") commenced in 1650, which gives an account of all the existing Irish clans and of the early populations that preceded the Milesian dynasty. It is a work of the highest importance, upon which all writers on Irish history draw as a principal source. Portions of it have been edited and translated by O'Donovan. He was also the transcriber of the *Chronicum Scotorum*, edited and translated by W. M. Hennessy in the Rolls Series (1866). From 1655–66 he assisted Sir James Ware [*q.v. Leinster* volume], in collecting and translating Irish *Annals* and other materials for his work on the antiquities and ecclesiastical history of Ireland, several of which are still extant. This venerable scholar and great master of Irish learning was wantonly murdered by a country squire at Dunflin, in Sligo, while resting in a wayside inn on his way to Dublin.

MAC HALE, John (1791–1881), Archbishop of Tuam, was born at Tubbernanne, in Mayo. He early attracted notice by his letters on *Church Establishment and Education*. He was the most prominent figure in Irish politics next to O'Connell, who referred to him as the "Lion of the Fold of Judah." He was celebrated as

L

a preacher both in England and in Italy.   He published
Irish translations of Moore's *Melodies*, the *Iliad* (i.–viii.),
and the *Pentateuch*.

O'CAROLAN, Turlough (1670–1738), poet and musician,
though born in Meath, spent his life in Co. Leitrim,
whither his parents, having lost all their possessions,
removed shortly after his birth.   Having lost his sight
from small-pox when a youth of sixteen, he adopted
the bardic profession.   He was the most popular and
favoured bard of his day.   His best-known pieces are
Gracey Nugent, Wild Mabel Kelly, and *Bridget Cruise.*
He was both poet and musician.   An incomplete
edition of his compositions was brought out in 1747
by his son, who was a teacher of the harp in London.
A marble bas-relief of his head by Hogan [*q.v. Leinster*
volume] is in St Patrick's Cathedral, Dublin.

O'CONOR, Charles, D.D. (1764–1828), antiquary and
librarian of Stowe, born at Belanagare and educated
at Rome.   He first attracted attention by his letters
Columbanus ad Hibernos (1810–13), in which he ad-
vocated the veto in the appointment of Catholic Bishops
in Ireland.   His great work, *Rerum Hibernicarum
Scriptores* (1814–26), containing first editions with
Latin translations of the principal Irish annals (Four
Masters, Ulster, Tigernach, Innisfallen, Boyle), though
marred by his defective knowledge of Irish, was an
immense undertaking, and one of undoubted utility.
He also published a *Descriptive Catalogue of the MSS.
in Stowe Library* (1818).   His *Life of Charles O'Conor
of Belanagare* (1796), the antiquary, his grandfather,
is of extreme rarity, having been suppressed on the
appearance of the first volume ; the second was destroyed in manuscript.

Ó DUBHAGÁIN, Seán (d. 1372), chief poet of the O'Kellys, was a native of Connaught. He is best known by his great *Topographical Poem* on the tribes and territories of Meath, Ulster, and Connaught at the time of the Anglo-Norman invasion. It was completed for the rest of Ireland by Giolla na Naomh Ó Huidhrin (d. 1420). As the work embodies many ancient traditions, it is of the greatest historical value. It was edited and translated by John O'Donovan in 1862. He also wrote chronological poems on the kings of Ireland.

O'FLAHERTY, Roderick (1629-1718), historian, was born at the Castle of Moycullen in Galway. His father, who was the head of the clan, dying when he was an infant, Roderick became a ward of the crown. In 1652 he was deprived of almost all the parental estates by the Parliamentarians, and reduced to penury. His long life was devoted to the history and antiquities of Ireland, which he studied under Duald MacFirbis [*q.v.*] and his friend John Lynch [*q.v.*]. His great work, *Ogygia seu Rerum Hibernicarum Chronologia* from the earliest times to 1684, appeared in 1685, dedicated to the Duke of York, afterwards James II. In reply to the strictures of Sir George Mackenzie, lord advocate of Scotland, he wrote *Ogygia Vindicated*, which lay in MS. until 1775, when it was published by Charles O'Conor (1710-91). His *Chorographical Description of West Connacht*, a valuable work written in Irish, was edited and translated in 1846 by James HARDIMAN (1782-1855), also a native of Galway, and author of the well-known *History of Galway* (1820) and *Irish Minstrelsy* (1831).

Ó HUIGINN, Tadhg *Dall* or the Blind (d. 1671),

L *

the most conspicuous Gaelic poet of his time, was a native of Sligo. He wrote many fine odes and poems addressed principally to the Maguires, Ó'Rourkes, and O'Connors, and other warring chiefs, ever exhorting them to unite against the common enemy. He was murdered, together with his wife and child, by a party of the O'Haras whom he had satirised. They were attainted for the crime and their lands forfeited to the king.

Ó NEACHTAIN, Seán (17th–18th cent.), Gaelic poet and romancist, was a native of Connaught. His spirited *Maggie Laidir*, and his beautiful *Elegy on Mary D'Este*, widow of James II., are the poems by which he is best known. He is also the author of two prose tales, *An Gleacuidhe Géaglonnach* or "the Strong-armed wrestler," and *Stair Eamoinn Úi Chlérigh*, "The History of Edmond O'Cleary," a satirical piece. His son Tadhg Ó Neachtain was the compiler of a valuable dictionary of the Irish language.

STOKES, Sir George Gabriel, 1st Baronet (1819–1903), mathematician and physicist, was born at Skreen, Co. Sligo, where his father was rector, and educated at Pembroke College, Cambridge, of which he subsequently became Master. In 1849 he was appointed Lucasian professor of mathematics at Cambridge, a post which he retained until his death. He was secretary of the Royal Society from 1854–85, and President 1885–90. He represented his university in Parliament from 1887–91. One of the greatest men of science of his time, he is said to have founded modern geodesy by his memoirs on the variation of gravity over the earth's surface (1849). His subsequent investigations were mainly in the field of optics. For his great discovery of the nature of fluorescence, communicated in a memoir *On the Change of Refrangibility of Light* (1852), he was awarded the Rumford Medal.

Sir George Gabriel Stokes

He also received the Prussian Order *Pour le Mérite* and the Arago Medal from the French Institute, and was created a baronet in 1889. His *Mathematical and Physical Papers* were collected in five volumes,

1880–1905, and a *Memoir and Scientific Correspondence*, 2 vols, 1907. The celebration of his jubilee at Cambridge in 1899 was an event in the scientific world. Delegates were sent by all the principal universities, academies, and scientific institutions. Honorary degrees were conferred, and a volume of *Memoirs* by eminent scientific men published in his honour.

WILDE, Sir William Robert Wills (1815–76), surgeon and antiquary, was born at Castlerea, Co. Roscommon, and studied at the universities of Dublin, Berlin, and Vienna. He was the founder of St Mark's Ophthalmic Hospital, Dublin (1844), and he also founded and edited the *Dublin Quarterly Journal of Medical Science*. For his labours on the Irish census he was knighted in 1864. His *Epidemic Ophthalmia* (1851), and *Aural Surgery* (1853), were works of capital importance. It is as an antiquary, however, that he is most widely known, particularly by his fine *Catalogue of the Antiquities in the Royal Irish Academy Collection* (1857–62), of which he was the curator, his *Boyne and Blackwater* (1849), and *Lough Corrib* (1867). His wife, Jane Francesca ELGEE (1826–96), was no less remarkable as a poet and folklorist. Over the pseudonym "Speranza" she contributed several striking political articles to the *Nation* newspaper, one of which *Jacta alea est* led to the charge against Charles Gavan Duffy for treason. Their son, Oscar WILDE (1856–1900), was the well-known poet and dramatist.

INDEX